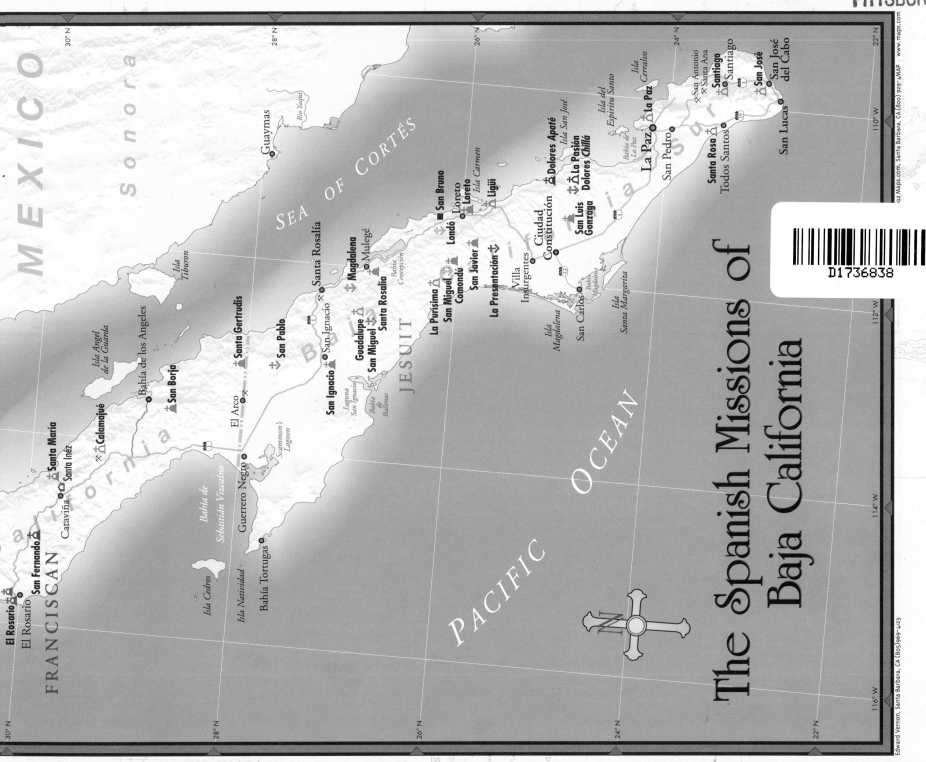

The Spanish Missions of Baja California

Edward Vernon, Santa Barbara, CA (805) 969-4123

D1736838

MEXICO

Sonora

Sea of Cortés

PACIFIC OCEAN

JESUIT

FRANCISCAN

Río Yaqui

Guaymas

Isla Tiburón

Isla Ángel de la Guarda

Bahía de los Ángeles

Isla Cedros

Isla Natividad

Bahía Tortugas

Bahía de Sebastián Vizcaíno

Scammon's Lagoon

Guerrero Negro

El Arco

Laguna San Ignacio

Bahía de Ballenas

San Bruno

Loreto

Liguí

Isla Carmen

Isla del Carmen

Londó

San Javier

La Presentación

Comondú

San Miguel

La Purísima

Magdalena

Mulegé

Bahía Concepción

Santa Rosalía

Santa Rosalia

San Ignacio

Guadalupe

San Miguel

San Pablo

Santa Gertrudis

San Borja

Calamajué

Cataviña

Santa María

Santa Inéz

San Fernando

San Rosario

El Rosario

Dolores Apaté

La Pasión

Dolores Chillá

Isla San José

San Luis Gonzaga

Ciudad Constitución

Villa Insurgentes

San Carlos

Isla Magdalena

Isla Margarita

Bahía Magdalena

Santa Margarita

Isla del Espíritu Santo

Isla Cerralvo

Bahía de La Paz

La Paz

San Pedro

Santa Rosa

Todos Santos

San Antonio

Santa Ana

Santiago

San José del Cabo

San Lucas

San José

Baja California Sur

22° N   24° N   26° N   28° N   30° N

110° W   112° W   114° W   116° W

N

www.maps.com

Las Misiones Antiguas

A Photographic Essay on The Missions

from Cape San Lucas to San Diego

Founded by the Jesuits, Franciscans, and Dominicans

*Barbara, my wife of so many years, has given me love and support
and always insisted that I proceed with my quest even though she had good
reason to ask that I stay home and personally give her the
attention and care that she deserves. How do I thank her for this?*

The sometimes nearly overwhelming task of completing this book was eased and made most enjoyable by the
wonderful corps of people who gave me information and encouragement. Some also provided new or old photographs or spent
valuable time to help educate me in the production and publishing of books. All were of great help and are mentioned in the
credits section; however, a few gave such important assistance that I want to specially recognize them:

Pancho Bareño of the mission museum in Loreto, who guided me to several hard-to-find sites and gave me
invaluable information to aid in the computer reconstruction of the mission at *Comondú*; my brother Clark, who
accompanied me to the most remote sites; Dr. Michael Mathes, who loaned me many photographs from his past
Baja California travels, and offered text suggestions and historical corrections; and Harry Crosby, who loaned me photographs but,
more importantly, gave his enthusiastic approval and encouragement to my project.
I was also fortunate to find Margaret Dodd of Santa Barbara, who made apt design suggestions, corrected my
grammar and punctuation, and performed her task of editing with great skill and good humor.

Las Misiones Antiguas

The Spanish Missions of Baja California*

1683 – 1855

Edward W. Vernon

* ALL BUT THE FINAL MISSION IN BAJA CALIFORNIA WERE FOUNDED BEFORE THE SPANISH WERE OVERTHROWN IN 1821.

Viejo Press, 729 Woodland Drive, Santa Barbara, CA 93108

Distribution by The University of New Mexico Press

Published with the assistance of a generous grant from
the California Mission Studies Association

Photographs of the missions under the control of INAH
(Loreto, San Javier, San Vicente Ferrer, and El Rosario)
have been included with their approval. *Reproducción
Autorzada por el Instituto Nacional de Antropología e Historia* .

Library of Congress Cataloging-in-Publication Data
Vernon, Edward W. 1926–
Las misiones antiguas : the Spanish missions of Baja California
1683-1855 / Edward W. Vernon
p. cm.
Includes bibliographical references and index.
ISBN 0-8263-3110-6
1. Missions, Spanish--Mexico--Baja California (Peninsula) 2. Catholic Church--Mexico--Baja California
(Peninsula)--History. 3. Spanish mission buildings--Mexico--Baja California (Peninsula)
4. Baja California (Mexico : Peninsula)--Church history. I. Title.
F1246.V47 2002   972'.202

Printed in Hong Kong

Las Misiones Antiguas   Contents   Baja California

Clockwise from upper left: El Camino Real south of San Borja; choir loft window, San Borja; elephant tree, near Santiago; San Javier bell tower.

LA CABEZA Y MADRE DE LAS MISIONES DE BAJA Y ALTA CALIFORNIA
The Head and Mother of the Missions of Baja and Alta California

This inscription is carved into the stone lintel above the impressive main entry of *Misión Nuestra Señora de Loreto* in the *pueblo* of the same name. Located on the Sea of Cortés, 300 miles north of the tip of the Baja California peninsula, the site was selected by Jesuit Padre Juan María de Salvatierra in the year 1697 for what became the first successful mission in the Spanish Californias.

As an *Alta California* schoolboy, I was taught that in 1769 Father Junípero Serra, a Catholic priest of the Franciscan order, came to San Diego after a rigorous trip from Mexico. There he founded what most Alta Californians think of as the first California mission, to enable the conversion of the numerous natives and commence colonization. Before Serra's death, he founded nine of the 21 missions that eventually spanned from San Diego to San Francisco, as well as one mid-peninsula Baja California mission called *Velicatá*. The Alta California establishments were an ambitious extension of the earlier chain of Jesuit missions that were initiated at Loreto.

Until I started to travel to Baja California, I was only vaguely aware of the mostly earlier, equally wonderful, and more numerous string of missions covering the length of the peninsula. As a matter of fact, the area that we *Norte Americanos* call "Baja" was settled long before "our" Califor-

nia; at that time the Baja California peninsula was called "California," and the area north of the peninsula, "Alta California."

All of the Baja California peninsula, most of Alta California, and Arizona, Colorado, New Mexico, and Texas were claimed as the property of Spain by the end of the 17th century. A permanent settlement for the Christianizing of the indigenous Californians was first attempted by Father Eusebio Kino and Admiral Atondo y Antillón. In 1683, they built a short-lived mission/fort at San Bruno, 20 miles north of Loreto. The mission period in Baja California lasted until the secularization order of 1834. By then, 30 missions plus numerous satellite farms, *visitas,* and *ranchos* were built on the peninsula. It was not until 1849, as part of the Mexican-American war settlement, that Alta California and most of the other southwestern states were separated from Mexico. The rich history of Baja California and its missions is an important part of the history and culture of what is now the state of California in the United States of America.

Traveling in Baja California to explore its missions is a rewarding experience because of the remoteness of many of the sites, the scant population, the marvelous desert and mountain scenery, and the privilege of seeing the Spanish missions in their original and "natural" setting uncontaminated by modern civilization. A few still function as churches, and formal services are offered occasionally to accommodate the surrounding small ranching communities, where many of the simple homes are thatch-roofed and the people are of friendly, simple, and honest demeanor.

The final and most developed location of every known mission has been visited and photographed by the author. In some areas, several locations for the same mission were visited, as in the case of *San Javier* and *Comondú*. However, as many missions were moved several times, the exact location of the earliest and all of the site(s) may not be known. Also included are photographs and information on three of the more important *visitas* that offer interesting remnants for exploration and photography.

In order to reach the places described, it was necessary to drive several thousand miles on the scenic and paved Highway 1 and to explore nearly 500 miles of backcountry dirt roads and trails using a high-clearance, four-wheel-drive vehicle. Several areas are inaccessible other than by foot or muleback, and to reach every site, it was necessary to visit one by motorcycle and one via the gulf coast by a local fisherman's *panga*.

In addition to portraying the many striking historic buildings and scenic locations, the author hopes to give the reader an understanding of the determination and faith required to establish missions in this arid, hostile terrain. Even though the disastrous effect of European civilization on the Indians and their environment is a tragic and poignant story, it is an integral part of the fascinating Spanish and Mexican mission era on the peninsula.

It is most thought-provoking to consider the remarkable edifices and the surrounding infrastructure of western civilization that were created under the extremely trying and difficult conditions. Also, it is important to have some understanding of the motivation and reasoning of the Spanish, the Catholic church, and the missionaries who were responsible for the enormous physical and cultural impact that forever changed this intriguing land.

The adventure of our travels, the supportive companionship of my friends, the willing guidance and assistance of the locals, and the thrill of finding standing ruins in isolated but often ruggedly beautiful mountains and desert are truly a privilege. I feel so fortunate to have been able to make this wonderful journey.

The belief, or perhaps the hope, that the Baja California peninsula was an island, persisted from the visits of the first European explorers in the early 16th century until well into the 18th century. A number of explorers probed the Sea of Cortés trying to find a shorter, more protected route to the Orient. Territorial expansion, religious proselytization, pearls, and piracy were among the other incentives that first spurred European interest—Portuguese, Spanish, Dutch and English—in the Baja California peninsula and the Sea of Cortés (Gulf of California).

Even though several times proven to be a peninsula, Baja California continued to be thought of as an island, and was named after the mythical land of California governed by beautiful Amazon Queen Calafia, as described by a romantic novel written in 1510.

New Spain, after the 1519–1521 conquest of Cortés, had developed into a profitable enterprise for the Crown because of the vast new lands claimed and the new subjects brought under the Spanish flag. The Catholic church too was accomplishing its goals by building numerous missions, acquiring large tracts of land, and most importantly, harvesting numerous heathen souls by baptizing and Christianizing the many different tribes of indigenous people.

Cortés, following his victory over the Aztecs in Mexico, became the major force in the development of New Spain for the Crown. He made extensive explorations, built permanent roads, and in 1522 built a shipyard and ships on the west coast of New Spain. In 1533, Cortés sponsored an exploration of the Gulf of California with his ships, the *San Lázaro* and the *Concepción*. On its initial voyage, the *Concepción*, under the command of Captain Diego Becerra, was seized by the crew, who killed the captain. After the mutiny, the ship and crew made their way to La Paz to reprovision and replenish their water supply, where 22 of the crew and their leader, the pilot Jiménez, were killed by hostile Indians. The surviving crew escaped with the ship and returned to mainland Mexico.

The discoverers of Baja California, the survivors of the *Concepción*, brought tales of beautiful pearls worn by the Indians and the great riches to be found in this new land. These tales soon spurred a series of explorations and pearling voyages to the peninsula that were to last for more than the next 200 years. In 1535, Cortés tried to colonize at La Paz, which was selected because of its proximity to the pearl beds, its beautiful bay, and its water supply. A large party, including soldiers, families, and livestock, survived for less than two years before lack of food, insufficient water for farming, and resentful natives forced them to abandon their colonization attempt and return to the mainland.

Ferdinand Magellan, during his famous 1519 westbound voyage, found a passage through the southern tip of the South American continent. He then proceeded westward across the southern Pacific Ocean to the Philippines, which he claimed for Spain. Subsequent military action to subdue the Philippines led, in 1565, to the establishment of regular naval service from Acapulco to Manila and return, to procure the exotic treasures of the Orient. This trade was conducted by Manila galleons, which often took a full year to complete a single round-trip of the grueling voyage.

The return trip was particularly difficult because the clumsy galleons made agonizingly slow progress eastward across the north Pacific into unfavorable winds and currents. By the time the California coast was reached, the crew was sorely depleted; water, fresh food, and rest were mandatory before continuation of the journey. Often one-half of the crew died from the rigors of the passage. At Cabo San Lucas, fresh water was available just 15 miles northeast of its southern tip, in a large palm-lined *estero* near the present village of San José. The wide open bay of San Bernabé, east of the estero, offered an excellent anchorage for the galleons, as well as for explorers and pirates.

The cove adjacent to the modern Mexican resort city of San Lucas, with a wall-like rock formation now known as Los Arcos, offered a prime hiding place for pirates and privateers, such as Thomas Cavendish of England. Many galleons were attacked and a few captured or sunk by the enemies of Spain, using this natural hiding place to await the approach of eastbound treasure-laden ships manned by weakened and often scurvy-stricken crews.

Not only did the lure of pearls, gold, and other treasures bring a stream of adventurers, but new lands and trade routes were sought by the European powers. Ships from England, Holland, as well as Spain joined the quest for land and riches. Juan Rodríguez Cabrillo, sailing under the Spanish flag, landed in La Paz in 1542 and sailed northward in the Sea of Cortés, then later turned southward to round the Cape and sail up the Alta California coast as far as the bay of Monterey. Cabrillo, who died near the Channel Islands off Santa Barbara while leading the expedition, was followed by men such as Sebastián Vizcaíno, who not only tried to establish a colony at La Paz in Baja California, but in 1602 led his small fleet of ships as far north as Cape Blanco at 48 degrees north on the Pacific coast.

The few colonization attempts of the period were unsuccessful primarily because of lack of sufficient water for agriculture. None of the pearling expeditions, which often included several large ships, small diving boats, many native divers, and in one case a crude diving bell, resulted in highly profitable ventures for the sponsors. The excessive cost of outfitting, the unpredictable gulf weather, the forbidding shoreline, and often unfriendly natives made these expeditions very hazardous and of questionable commercial value.

It was not until 1683 that a land expedition was undertaken by the Spanish to determine the suitability of the area for settlement and for religious conversion. Padre Eusebio

Francisco Kino and Admiral Isidro de Atondo y Antillón, and their mounted and armored party of 50 soldiers and 100 loyal Indians from the mainland, established a base near San Bruno Bay, 20 miles north of Loreto. They used this short-lived mission/fort to launch expeditions to explore the peninsula until a route was found over the Sierra Giganta to the Pacific Ocean at Punta San Juanico, north of Magdalena Bay. The sites of the future missions of *Comondú* and *La Purísima*,

and the *visita* of *Londo,* were also found. The Kino/Atondo force was driven from its gulfside fort in early 1685 by lack of water and the difficulty in obtaining supplies from the mainland. A successful and permanent mission and colony finally gained a foothold on the fabled but hostile terrain of the Baja California peninsula more than 150 years after Cortés's first colonization attempt, when *Misión Nuestra Señora de Loreto* was established by Father Juan María de Salvatierra in 1697.

The Indians

At the time of the arrival of the Spanish, the Baja California peninsula was home to 40,000 to 50,000[*] Indians composed of four major language groups—*Yuman, Cochimí, Guaycura,* and *Pericú*—plus many subgroups, each with its separate and different dialect. About 10,000 of these natives lived in the northern coastal area (later the Dominican-developed lands), with the balance living in the southern two-thirds of the peninsula. These aborigines—with the exception of the natives living in the northernmost part of the peninsula and the area surrounding the Colorado River delta—were some of the most primitive of the indigenous population in North America.

The Indians, who lived by hunting and gathering, roamed

[*] SEE NOTE AT END OF SECTION REGARDING SOURCES OF POPULATION STATISTICS.

in small groups of 30 to 80, called *rancherías.* They searched widely, usually about a familiar water source, to find game, including snakes and lizards, food plants and roots, and fish and shellfish when near the gulf or sea. Constant movement was necessary to allow the gathering of seasonally available food in areas not recently harvested. No permanent homes were built, and they slept on the ground without shelter except for an occasional brush hut. Until trained by the padres, no pottery was made by the natives, and water was carried in animal bladders. Fiber-net sacks were woven as totes and also used as fish nets. Their weapons consisted of bows and arrows, lances, and bone or shell knives.

The men were nude but wore decorative bits of bone, shells, and other natural trinkets in their hair and sometimes on their wrists or ankles. The women wore woven plant-fiber aprons, and similarly made hair nets were used by both sexes. Even though thought of as "barbaric," "lazy," "uncouth and ungrateful" (Baegert), the padres were eager to save the Indian's souls that were "precious as pearls" (Piccolo).

It is interesting to contemplate that the peninsula could support such a large number of inhabitants (approximately one person per square mile) living by the most basic means, hunting and gathering without the cultivation of crops, and having no domestic animals. Contrast this with the ever-present shortages of food experienced by both the greatly reduced native population and the missionaries during nearly 80 years of development of the Jesuit era. Vigorous efforts were made to farm and ranch—soil was imported in strategic areas and extensive irrigation systems developed. Herds of cattle, goats, and sheep were established. In spite of this, there simply was not enough food produced to feed the populace. A constant flow of foodstuffs shipped across the gulf from mainland New Spain was always needed to prevent starvation. In times of severe shortages, it was necessary to encourage the mission Indians to return to the wild and resume their traditional food-gathering techniques. Unfortunately this was not always successful, as "reduction" had taken away their skills of subsisting from the creatures and plants native to the peninsula. A poignant story concerning the plight of the Indians in these periods of famine was told

by Father Serra after his 1768 trek to visit all the missions, to determine what church possessions could be requisitioned for the new missions to be established in Alta California. Serra wrote, "…there I talked to some ten families of Indians, …they told me with much sorrow that they were from the Mission Guadalupe; and that the father, for want of provisions, had found himself obliged to send them out to the mountains to seek food, and as they were not used to this their hardship was great, particularly in seeing their babies suffer and hearing them cry…." Serra gave them what food he could spare and told them that they might get food from a provisioning ship soon due at Loreto.

Even though food was always a problem, the most debilitating factor was the introduction of European diseases. The Indians were newly exposed to smallpox, typhus, measles, and syphilis. As they had no immunity to these diseases, the population decreased with alarming rapidity. The spread of disease was exacerbated by the closeness of mission life. Instead of being scattered throughout the countryside, village life at the mission made everyday contact common and the spread of disease was abetted. Further, the padres insisted that single girls and women live in large barracks-like single-room sleeping quarters with minimal sanitary facilities. Although this was done to protect the women and to isolate them from the Spanish soldiers, the practice almost insured that any communicable diseases would quickly be spread.

The mission records, although incomplete, indicate the disasterous effect of disease on the indigenous population. Derived statistics indicate that the 30,000 to 40,000 aboriginals who occupied the Jesuit territories (the southern two-thirds of the peninsula) on the arrival of the Europeans, shrank to fewer than 7,000, as shown by the census taken at the Jesuits' expulsion in 1768. The Dominican era was equally disastrous to the Indians; the northern missions recorded a population loss of 75 percent in the years from 1780 to 1836. By 1850, there were no native *Pericú, Guaycura,* or *Cochimí* in the southern two-thirds of the peninsula. The few remaining Indians were of the *Yuman* tribes, and occupied the foothills of the San Pedro Mártir and Sierra Juárez ranges as well as the Colorado desert area. The approximately 1,200 Indians who now live in these same lands survive perhaps because their fiercely independent ancestors fled to the mountains and desert far from the life-threatening mission environment.

The relationship of the Jesuits with the Indians seems to have been positive at most of the missions, and when the Jesuits were forced to leave in 1768, by the expulsion order, many devout, faithful, and grieving Indians assembled at Loreto to bid their mentors good-by. However, even those dedicated priests had been set upon by the rebellious *Pericú,* who raided and sacked the four southern missions and killed two padres in the revolt of 1734. The Dominicans had their problems too, and many of the coastal missions were fre-quently attacked by the warlike Colorado delta Indians. At *Misión Santo Tomás,* two priests were murdered by local Indians within one year.

The Indians' response to "reduction" varied. Some adapted to mission life and quite peacefully lived under the guidance and supervision of the padres, even though the life was very different from their prior existence. The padres demanded hard work both in the fields and in building the mission infrastructure. The Indians were taught crafts and trades, food and education were furnished when possible, and in the Dominican era, village life was provided in return for loss of freedom. Most importantly, from the viewpoint of the padres, the Indians were given frequent lessons in Catholic dogma and doctrine to help them attain the benefits of Christianity.

Other tribal groups and individuals would not give up their traditional way of living, and resisted efforts to force them to accept mission life in every possible way. Some took refuge in remote areas, others raided the missions and the mission Indians. Those who ran away after being "reduced" made themselves subject to forcible return and sometimes corporal punishment.

The overwhelming tragedy of the Baja California missions is that imported diseases so decimated the indigenous population that there were virtually no survivors to carry on life in the rural village style envisioned by the padres.

Even though the Indians' sad fate was inevitable as soon as Europeans discovered the peninsula, it is ironic that the plight of the Indians was brought to them by well-intentioned and devout priests, who came not only to save the souls of the heathen, but also to teach them to survive in the modern world. Many of the Christian religious believe that this tremendous undertaking was necessary and worthwhile because the missionaries' self-sacrificing work, while not successful in a material way, did insure that thousands of heathens would be admitted to the Kingdom of Heaven.

DR MICHAEL MATHES, BAJA CALIFORNIA AUTHORITY, HAS PUBLISHED STUDIES CONCLUDING THAT THE POPULATION OF THE JESUIT AREA DID NOT EXCEED 30,000. ROBERT H. JACKSON, IN THE SPANISH BORDERLANDS SOURCE BOOK, DERIVES A POPULATION OF 41,500 FOR THIS AREA.

The Missionaries

Three orders of the Catholic church—the Jesuits, Franciscans, and Dominicans—were called upon, and eagerly accepted, the unknown and awesome responsibility to make Christians of and "reduce" the estimated 50,000 natives on the Baja California peninsula from wild, free, "heathen" hunter-gatherers to Christian, European-like, village farm dwellers. Further, in addition to training and indoctrinating the Indians into the Catholic faith, the padres were to educate and train them in skills that would be useful in the community and as loyal subjects of the King of Spain.

The Jesuits, under Father Juan María de Salvatierra, gained permission to take responsibility for the large indigenous population of the peninsula in 1697 after successfully establishing dozens of missions in New Spain. Father Salvatierra and his early fellow missionaries, such as Ugarte and Piccolo as well as other Jesuits to follow, were a very special kind of men. First of all, most came from aristocratic, powerful, and privileged families. They had received the best education that Europe could offer, and were trained not only in theology and philosophy but were also schooled in mathematics, cartography, astronomy, and other high-level disciplines of the day. They left comfortable positions of prestige and influence within the church in Europe to eagerly take on a life of privation, danger, and physical discomfort in order to civilize, and most importantly, save the souls of the Indians by teaching them the word of God.

Obviously these were men of great faith and determination, but to succeed they also had to learn to be exceptional leaders as well as frontiersmen, developing essential skills in architecture, construction, farming, cattle ranching, medicine, and whatever was required to build and operate a church, village, and farm—all of which made up a mission—in one of the most hostile terrains of the world. They took on this formidable task with only a bare minimum of funds for supplies and almost no military support, and entered the unknown to pursue what they considered to be their God-mandated task.

Not only were the Jesuits asked to secure the new lands for church and king, but no monies from the royal treasury were allocated for the endeavor. To finance the missions, the Jesuits established the "Pious Fund"; wealthy donors were asked to contribute to a trust established to support the missionary effort in the new and intriguing land of California. Often a donor would contribute a sum large enough to found a particular mission (that might be named in honor of the donor), with a remainder to draw interest to provide an annual maintenance income. The fund was also used to pay the soldiers, as the unique theocracy granted the padres did not provide for a military force funded by the king.

Loreto, home of the mother mission, became the seat of government, a *presidio,* distribution center, Indian encampment, and *pueblo.* During the time of the Jesuits, an exceptional arrangement was in place whereby the military and civil government were under the control of the missionaries and administered from Loreto.

At the outlying missions, often a single padre was stationed with only one servant or aide for companionship and a soldier for protection. The priest's life was lonely and difficult, as it was necessary that he learn the local native dialect before beginning the tasks of religious training and building

the infrastructure of the mission. The remarkable complexes that were built, many times with a single craftsman and the padre to instruct the native laborers, attest to the skills and talents that were developed by these unusual men.

The devoted Jesuits seemed to engender respect and admiration from their many converts. Nevertheless, they were victims of the largest and most organized Indian revolt of the mission era. The tremendous change in culture and lifestyle required by the padres, particularly the ban on polygamy, infuriated the Indians. In October 1734, the warlike *Pericú* attacked the four southern missions. They sacked and destroyed the missions at *San José, La Paz, Santiago,* and *Todos Santos*—two priests, Fathers Carranco and Tamaral, were murdered. In spite of bringing in a force of well-armed soldiers and loyal Indians from the mainland, it took three years to subdue the revolt.

During the Jesuit era, which ended in 1768, 18 missions and many visiting stations were built spanning from the tip of the peninsula at San José del Cabo to the last Jesuit structure at Santa María, 600 miles to the north. On the arrival of Father Salvatierra in 1697, there were an estimated 30,000 to 40,000 natives in the southern two-thirds of the peninsula—the area that was developed by the Jesuits. By the time of their departure, there were fewer than 7,000 natives recorded in a census. The rapid decline was due to the natives' almost total lack of immunity to the diseases brought to the peninsula by the Europeans.

In June 1767, orders from Charles III, King of Spain, expelled all Jesuits from the Spanish dominions. Political considerations in Europe and the Jesuits' almost unlimited power in the Americas brought on the drastic edict. After toiling 70 years to establish civilization in a harsh rock- and thorn-filled wilderness, and after converting thousands of heathens to Christianity, the 16 Jesuits on the peninsula were ordered to report to Loreto, where they were put under military guard. Their February 5, 1768 departure on the ship *Concepción* was witnessed by many grieving converts. Villagers and soldiers as well as Indians lined the beach below the mission at Loreto to bid farewell to the well-loved and respected padres.

Immediately following the expulsion, the military took over the administration of the missions. The system that was already reeling from loss of converts due to disease suffered drastically from the incompetent and corrupt rule of the soldier-*comisionados* who were appointed to operate the missions until the arrival of the priests from the Franciscan order. By that time, mission fields were untended, religious articles were missing, lost, or stolen; many Indians had deserted, and their religious practices, training, and education had been totally neglected.

The Franciscans, who were chosen to replace the Jesuits, assembled at *Loreto* on April 1, 1768. Father Junípero Serra, president of the California missions, assumed his responsibilities at *Loreto,* aided by Father Fernando Parrón. The other Franciscans were assigned to their posts, one at each of the 15 remaining missions from *Misión San José del Cabo,* 200 miles to the south, to *Misión Santa María,* 400 miles to the north.

The morning after meeting in *Loreto,* the 15 priests assigned to the outlying missions started walking 23 miles up a steep rocky trail to *Misión San Javier,* high in the Sierra Giganta. They completed the long climb up a very difficult twisting canyon trail in a single day. These men were not only faithful and devout but they were determined and physically tough!

After a night's rest at *San Javier,* they started on their individual treks, probably with a single soldier for each padre, a servant, and some supplies carried by muleback. They were to walk into an unknown land, over El Camino Real, little more than a pack-animal trail through the thick cactus and brush, some as far as 400 miles, to take over their assigned mission. There they would meet a group of Indians whose language they did not know, and further become responsible for all the spiritual and temporal needs of their charges. It is amazing to realize that these men took on the daunting responsibilities that they were assigned willingly and eagerly.

The Franciscan stay in Baja California, until 1773, was not marked by great achievements, as they were forced to struggle to reestablish the authority and respect that had vanished with the departure of the Jesuits. Only one new mission was established—*San Fernando*—to replace the poorly located *Misión Santa María*. The site of the new mission, with the Indian place name of *Velicatá,* was where Father Serra, in 1769, met with Captain Gaspar de Portolá to commence their well-known overland trek to San Diego to found the first mission in *Alta California*. Serra stayed on in Alta California to become famous for his leadership role in this northward extension of the missions to realize the ambitions of the church, and block the Russian advances to the south by colonizing this marvelous land for Spain.

As it became evident that the task of mission building in Alta California would require all of the resources of the Franciscans, it was also apparent that additional facilities were needed to link the Baja California missions with the new Franciscan establishment at San Diego. This would provide an overland supply route to service the fledgling Alta California missions, and establish new facilities for the Christianization of the Indians in the 240 miles of yet untouched coastal lands between *Velicatá* and San Diego. The friars of the Dominican order were given, and gladly accepted, this assignment.

The first Dominican mission was constructed in 1774 and named *Nuestra Señora del Rosario*. It was sited on the Pacific coast 40 miles north of the Franciscan mission at *Velicatá*. Eight additional missions were founded by the Dominicans; five were located near the Pacific coast, spanning the 200 miles between El Rosario and San Diego. One mountain

mission was built in the foothills of the Sierra San Pedro Mártir, another mission was built to protect a pass leading to the Colorado River delta, and the final Dominican construction was *Guadalupe del Norte* in a fertile valley 30 miles northeast of the present town of Ensenada.

The Dominicans had accepted a difficult task, as all of the missions to the south had badly deteriorated and their population had shrunk from introduced diseases. In spite of these problems, ambitious building projects were undertaken, old buildings refurbished, and new structures, some of stone, erected at many of the sites previously established by the Jesuits. All of the new Dominican missions were built of adobe.

A strong military presence was needed throughout the northern Dominican territory, as the natives of the upper peninsula seemed to be quite independent and often resisted missionization. The soldiers were used as scouts, explorers, and to insure security and enforce discipline. Further, they were not under the direct control of the priests, as were the soldiers of the Jesuits. The soldiers took their orders from the governor of California, and conducted many explorations to discover lands suitable for colonization and trade as well as new missions.

The attitude of the Dominicans toward the Indians was stern and domineering. Father Vicente Mora, the first Dominican president (1773–1781), issued regulations that called for "…a monastic life for neophytes, and included a demand for swift and sure punishment for all offences such as failure to attend religious services,…a complete segregation of the sexes except for spouses, and the elimination of profane (nonreligious) singing and all forms of recreation such as dancing or wrestling…which the Indians had practiced as gentiles." Meigs, after interviewing many of the descendants of the mission Indians, declared that whipping was a common practice even for minor offences. Father Englehardt, the Franciscan historian, comments on this form of discipline by quoting a letter from Father Apolinario, in 1796, addressed to the governor, protesting the limit of 25 lashes. He says, "…I do not know how it is that the paternal jurisdiction…should extend only to twenty-five lashes, for we see every day a father at times inflicts a slight punishment, and at other times a grave chastisement according as the misdeed demands. Can it foresooth be said that such a father does not love his sons?…In the second place, the motive for running away does not, as your Honor says, rise from too much chastising. Considering the character of these Indians, I dare say that they run away for lack of punishment rather than punishing them in keeping with the guilt."

The missionaries pictured themselves as stern but righteous parents with the responsibility to guide and mold the Indians into their proper place in mission and Spanish society. Although their enforcement of discipline may seem harsh it must be noted that at this time in history, whipping as a method of punishment was often used throughout Europe and America.

The clergy, the Spanish, and other Europeans were called *gente de razón,* people who lived as Europeans, while the Indians were regarded as gentiles or heathen up to the time they began instruction in the Catholic faith, when they became "neophytes." A neophyte was almost never elevated to the status of *gente de razón.* In spite of the attitude that the Indians were inferior and justly made subservient to the regulations of the church, the padres did their best and sometimes gave their lives to care for them. They provided food and clothing, taught them useful crafts, and educated and trained them in European morals and Catholicism.

At several missions, the priests used their knowledge of "modern" medicine to save their Indians from smallpox by an inoculation technique called "variolation." A pustule on an infected person was lanced and the live "serum" transferred to the healthy but at-risk Indian, by scratching the skin. This technique was widely used at *San Ignacio,* where hundreds of Indians were saved from the almost always fatal disease.

Even with the problems in obtaining sufficient numbers of Indian workers, caused by loss due to disease, many of the mission compounds were extensive and the amount of land cultivated impressive. Fortunately, most of the new Dominican missions were located in areas well-suited to farming and ranching. Orchards and gardens were developed, thousands of acres were devoted to the raising of wheat and other grains, large herds of livestock were tended, and the sea offered its bounty of fish and shellfish. The trapping of otters for their skins became an important commercial endeavor, as did the sometimes illegal trade with passing sailing ships.

In spite of the massive amount of labor expended in developing the mission lands, the decline of the system was sadly rapid. Disease quickly thinned the Indian population. The secularization order of 1834, which in Baja California was not applied until several years later, had little effect as, by the time of its enforced application, the missions were virtually depleted of converts and many sites were nearly deserted.

The peninsular area south of El Rosario had also been under Dominican administration. Although the Dominicans completed or made beautiful additions to the buildings and stone churches commenced by the Jesuits, the decline in Indian population began earlier in the south and the abandonment of the missions took place sooner than in the north. Some pueblos, such as Loreto, San Ignacio, and Todos Santos, struggled to survive, and the mission chapels served as parish churches to their small communities of descendants of the soldiers and immigrants from Mexico.

By 1841, there were only six missionaries to serve the surviving churches that spanned 800 miles from the Cape to San Diego. The Indian population at this time had dwindled to a few families living at the deserted coastal missions and those who populated the area from Santa Catarina east to the Colorado River.

The last Dominican missionary on the peninsula, an energetic and strong-willed man with a scandalous reputation, Father Gabriel González, departed from Baja California in 1855 after serving for 30 years. A few of the missions survived as parish churches, others furnished facilities for worship and an occasional service when a passing priest was available. Most, however, were simply deserted to be picked over by treasure seekers, used as barns, or abandoned until they melted to adobe mounds or crumbled to rock heaps as a result of the onslaught of the elements and time.

It is thought-provoking to realize that the 155 years of heartbreaking and well-intentioned efforts by the padres to bring the Indians into the civilized world, driven by faith, determination, and courage, are now represented by only a handful of faithful natives in the northeast corner of Baja California, a few standing churches, and lonely deserted sites marked by deteriorating walls or mounds of adobe and stone rubble. There are but a few stone churches, adobe ruins, old water systems and other deteriorating structures as the physical remnants of an era that was most important to the development of the Californias. The effects on the Indians of the padres' efforts and the spiritual and cultural benefits of Baja California's missionization are left to the reader to ponder.

Las Misiones Antiguas — Missions Guide — Baja California

DATE/NAME	FOUNDER	KEY FACTS	LOCATION	PRESENT CONDITION
JESUIT				
1683 – San Bruno 1685 (mission/fort)	Eusebio Francisco Kino (Italy)	1st mission attempt (failed)	N 26° 13.071' W 111° 22.724' On gulf, 20 miles N of Loreto	Rock breastworks outline remains
1697 – Nuestra Señora de 1829 Loreto de *Conchó*	Juan María de Salvatierra (Italy)	1st successful Baja/Alta mission	N 26° 00.641' W 110° 20.592' On Loreto plaza	Restored stone church; museum adjacent
1699 – San Francisco Javier 1817 de *Viggé-Biaundó*	Francisco María Piccolo (Sicily)	1st site 5 miles NE near Rancho Viejo	N 25° 51.663' W 111° 32.627' 23 mi. SW of Loreto in Sierra	Beautiful stone church in thatch-roofed village
1699 – Visita San Juan 1750 Bautista de *Londó*	Salvatierra/Piccolo	Kino-Atondo expedition site	N 26° 13.501' W 111° 28.405' 20 mi. N of Loreto on highway	Stone wall/corner; partial ceiling arc
1705 – San Juan Bautista 1721 de *Ligüí*	Pedro de Ugarte (Mexico)	Abandoned 1721; Indians to *Dolores*	N 25° 44.334' W 111° 15.874' 20 mi. S of Loreto on gulf	Destroyed by flood; foundation parts only
1705 – Santa Rosalía 1828 de *Mulegé*	Juan Manuel de Basaldúa (Spain)	Best watered mission; frequently restored	N 26° 53.227' W 111° 59.170' S bank of river at *Mulegé*	Large rebuilt stone church/service buildings
1708 – San José de *Comondú* 1827	Julián de Mayorga (Mexico)	Largest mission; verdant oasis canyon	N 26° 03.618' W 111° 49.315' 70 miles N of Cd. Constitución	Stone chapel, garden, & many ruins
1720 – La Purísima Concepción 1822 de *Cadegomó*	Nicolás Tamaral (Italy)	Lovely palm-lined canyon, live stream	N 26° 11.426' W 112° 04.377' 80 mi. NW of Cd. Constitución	Village walls from mission ruins; tombs remain
1720 – Nuestra Señora del Pilar 1748 de la Paz *Airapí*	Jaime Bravo (Spain) Juan de Ugarte (Hond.)	Abandoned after 1734 *Pericú* rebellion	N 24° 09.703' W 110° 18.782' City of La Paz plaza	No remnants; modern church near site

Las Misiones Antiguas Missions Guide Baja California

DATE/NAME	FOUNDER	KEY FACTS	LOCATION	PRESENT CONDITION
JESUIT *(continued)*				
1720 – N. S. de Guadalupe 1795 de *Huasinapí*	Everardo Helen (Germany)	Lumber for ship *El Triunfo*	N 26° 55.086' W 112° 24.393' 28 miles W of Mulegé	Stone mission wall & corrals on site
1721 – N. S. de los Dolores 1741 de *Apaté*	Clemente Guillén (Mexico)	Moved inland to *Chillá* in 1741	N 25° 03.343' W 110° 53.055' NW of La Paz on gulf	2nd site ruins; dam, *pila* & cave above *arroyo*
1724 – Santiago el Apóstol 1795 *Aiñiní*	Ignacio María Nápoli (Italy)	Destroyed by *Pericú*, 1734	N 23° 28.516' W 109° 43.066' In village "South"	No mission ruins; modern church on last site
1728 – Nuestro Sr. San Ignacio 1840 de *Kadakaamán*	Juan Bautista de Luyando (Mexico)	Productive; had consistent water	N 27° 17.023' W 112° 53.905' ½ mile S of Highway 1	Beautifully preserved stone church on plaza
1730 – San José del Cabo 1840 *Añuití*	Nicolás Tamaral (Spain)	Tamaral killed by *Pericú*, 1734	N 23° 02.947' W 109° 41.538' Highway 1, South Cape	No remnants; new church on last site
1733 – Santa Rosa de las Palmas 1825? Renamed Pilar 1748	Sigismundo Taraval (Italy)	Burned by *Pericú*, 1734; La Paz Indians imported	N 23° 27.621' W 110° 13.115' 1 mi. N of Todos Santos	Chapel built on first mission ruins in 1970
1737 – San Luis Gonzaga 1768 *Chiriyaqui*	Lamberto Hostell (Germany)	Became inn & cattle ranch headquarters	N 24° 54.518' W 111° 17.429' 28 miles SE of Cd. Constitution	Stone church, colonial mansion, dam
1740 – Visita San Pablo 1780 (Dolores del Norte)	Fernando Consag (Croatia)	*Visita* for San Ignacio; cave art area	N 27°48.50' W 113°15.10' (est.) In Arroyo de San Pablo	3-room adobe ruins; water system
1741 – Nuestra Señora de los 1768 Dolores *Chillá*	Lamberto Hostell (Germany)	*Vis.* La Pasión; renamed Dolores *Chillá* 1741	N 24° 53.280' W 111° 01.878' 16 miles from S. L. Gonzaga	Heap of stone rubble; *acequia* & *pila* nearby

Las Misiones Antiguas Missions Guide Baja California

DATE/NAME	FOUNDER	KEY FACTS	LOCATION	PRESENT CONDITION
JESUIT *(continued)*				
1751 – Santa Gertrudis 1822 de *Cadacamán*	Jorge Retz (Germany)	Irrigation canals & stone corrals remain	N 28° 03.085' W 113° 05.083' 15 miles SE of El Arco	Stone church; separate bell tower
1762 – San Francisco de Borja 1818 *Adac*	Retz, Wenceslaus Linck (Bohemia)	Original irrigation & fields in use	N 28° 45.104' W 110° 03.552' 21 miles E of Rosarito	Stone church, adobe ruins, spring & *pila*
1766 – Visita de *Calamajué* 1767	V. Arnés (Spain) Juan Díez (Mexico)	Bad water, abandoned to *Santa María*	N 29° 25.255' W 114° 11.698' 10 miles E of Laguna Chapala	Adobe heaps trace 4 bldgs; stone corrals
1767 – Santa María de L. A. 1769 *Cabujakaamung*	Victoriano Arnés	Last Jesuit mission; remote location	N 29° 43.888' W 114° 32.821' 15 miles E of Cataviña	Adobe end walls standing in 1999
FRANCISCAN				
1769 – San Fernando Rey 1818 de *Velicatá*	Junípero Serra (Spain)	1st Franciscan mission; Serra/Portolá start	N 29° 58.319' W 115° 14.180' 30 miles E of El Rosario	Adobe half walls, long *acequia*, petroglyphs
1769 – Visita de la Presentación 1817	Francisco Palóu	In narrow canyon with water & palms	N 23° 43.956' W 111° 32.575' 10 miles S of San Javier	Stone chapel, storeroom walls, corral, *pila*
DOMINICAN				
1774 – N. S. del Rosario 1832 de *Viñadaco*	Vicente Mora Francisco Galisteo	1st Dominican msn; 2nd site near river	N 30° 04.010' W 115° 43.098' N 30° 02.485' W 115° 44.335'	Deteriorating adobe walls at both sites
1774 – Visita San José 1828 de Magdalena	Joaquín Valero	Fertile canyon with terraced huertas	N 27° 03.834' W 112° 13.292' 17 miles NW of *Mulegé*	Stone chapel face & walls; *casa* foundations

Las Misiones Antiguas   Missions Guide   Baja California

DATE/NAME	FOUNDER	KEY FACTS	LOCATION	PRESENT CONDITION
DOMINICAN (*continued*)				
1775 – Santo Domingo 　1839　de la Frontera	Manuel García Miguel Hidalgo	2nd Dominican mission	N 30° 46.249' W 115° 56.204' 11 mi. to sea from canyon site	Adobe half walls; next to modern church
1780 – San Vicente Ferrer 　1833	Joaquín Valero Miguel Hidalgo	Frontier fort; partial restoration in 1997	N 31° 19.375' W 116° 15.547' Near highway, 10 miles from sea	Adobe ends of church standing
1787 – San Miguel Arcángel 　1833　de la Frontera	Luis Sales	4th Dominican msn.; display on site	N 32° 05.679' W 116° 51.314' At La Misión beside school	Minor wall fragments above river
1791 – Santo Tomás 　1849　de Aquino	José Loriente	5th Dominican msn.; 1850 Baja capital	N 31° 33.513' W 116° 24.817' 200 yards SE of Highway 1	Adobe mound of last site near olive grove
1794 – San Pedro Mártir 　1824　de Verona	José Loriente	Only sierra Dominican mission	N 30° 47.403' W 115° 28.325' 20 miles SE of Meling Ranch	Stone perimeter walls, water ditches
1797 – Santa Catalina 　1840　Virgen y Mártir	José Loriente	On *Paipai* Indian reservation	N 31° 39.483' W 115° 49.752' 50 miles SE of Ensenada	Discernable foundation outline
1817 – El Descanso 　1834	Tomás de Ahumada	Next to nursery; new church on site	N 23° 12.281' W 116° 54.323' S of Tijuana at El Descanso	Tile floor, melted adobe mounds
1825 – Nuestra Señora del Pilar 　1840	Gabriel González (?) (Mexico)	Moved from 1 mile north and restarted	N 23° 26.982' W 110° 13.523' On Todos Santos plaza	New plaza church foyer is 1825 chapel
1834 – Nuestra Señora 　1840　de Guadalupe Nte.	Félix Caballero	Destroyed by Indians; 1905 Russ. settlement	N 32° 05.445' W 116° 34.571' In village of El Povenir	Mound behind school; in productive agric. valley

The Spanish Missions of Baja California

CROSBY

El Camino Real, the lifeline that connected all of the missions, in some places cuts a broad path across the rocky desert terrain and in others is only a narrow, barely discernable trail. This historic pathway stirs the imagination to picture the tremendous difficulties experienced to bring western civilization to the harsh land of the peninsula.

1683 – 1685

San Bruno

THE FORTIFICATION OF THE KINO-ATONDO EXPEDITION

*N 26º 13.071'   W 111º 22.724'

*GPS LOCATION OF SAN BRUNO BAY

San Bruno

PLOCH, 1998

"A contrary wind blew and hence we could not land at San Bruno on its half bay." – Father Salvatierra, Sunday, October 13, 1697

San Bruno

Isidro de Atondo y Antillón, the governor of Sinaloa, was appointed admiral of the Californias in 1678 and given the responsibility of exploring and settling the intriguing land of the Baja California peninsula. Accompanied by Father Eusebio Kino, the famed Jesuit missionary, the expedition sailed to the present La Paz early in 1683.

A settlement was not successful as conflict arose with the natives, ending with a number of Indians being "massacred." This incident bred a long-lasting distrust of the Spanish and negatively affected later efforts to colonize the area.

The Kino-Atondo party was forced to search for a more suitable site and selected the bay and *arroyo* of San Bruno. The expedition landed there, 20 miles north of the future site of Loreto, in

Northwest of the point of land marking "the half bay of San Bruno," the location of the mission/fort beyond the estero may be seen. Londó is about 8 miles up this same broad wash and the Sierra Giganta rise sharply in the distance.

Left: *This small bay at the mouth of the San Bruno arroyo was the probable landing place of the Kino-Atondo party. Fourteen years later, Father Salvatierra, in search of a proper location for his mission, was blown past this unprotected anchorage and took refuge in Concepción Bay. A few days later, Salvatierra's party returned to San Bruno but believed it to be unsatisfactory for their purposes. They then sailed on to San Dionisio Bay, where they landed to establish Misión Nuestra Señora de Loreto.*

San Bruno

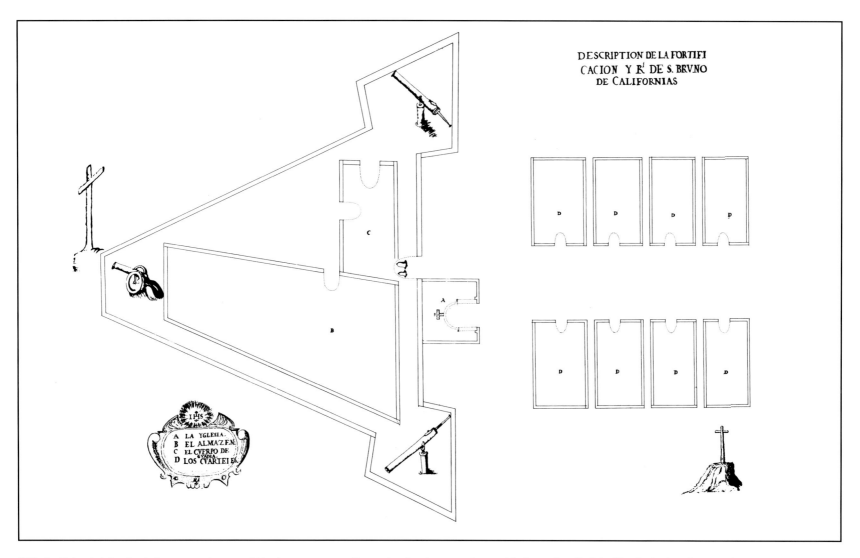

DESCRIPTION DE LA FORTIFI
CACION Y R! DE S. BRVNO
DE CALIFORNIAS

IHS

A LA YGLESIA.
B EL ALMAZEN.
C EL CVERPO DE GVARDIA
D LOS CVARTELES.

This fanciful period drawing indicates several rooms within the structure as well as a chapel and quarters just outside the north wall of the "fort." As the sides are only 70 feet long, the function of the enclosed area may have been for storage and defense of provisions. The space indicated as the chapel and quarters is a rocky irregular ridge that apparently was not graded for the uses suggested by the drawing. No trace of buildings or building materials were found in the chapel/quarters area during a 1999 examination of the site.

San Bruno

October 1683. A few miles inland, on the toe of a low promontory near the Sea of Cortés, a camp was established. The primary goals of the expedition were to cross the peninsula, explore the surroundings of Magdalena Bay, determine the suitability of the area for colonization, and indoctrinate the natives into the Catholic faith.

The party was equipped as a substantial military expeditionary force. Nearly 30 soldiers and, according to historian Michael Mathes' translation of *The Kino-Atondo Diary*, "…also aforesaid Father Rector Eusebio, a surgeon, Josef de Castro y Mendoza, Francisco Santiago, a muleteer, Diego de la Cruz, a slave, nine Christian Indians from New Spain, five armored horses which were led by halter, thirty saddle horses…twenty mules laden with provisions and war material,…and twenty-two mules in reserve." This made a most formidable troop!

Above left: *The 10-foot diameter "gun emplacement" at the apex of the fortification overlooks the valley as it slopes toward the sea.*

Left: *The low sides of the fort were made of a soft conglomerate rock piled to a height of 4 or 5 feet. Even though now overgrown with desert shrubs and cactus, the rocky mounds still clearly define the perimeter.*

San Bruno

A strategic hilltop position was selected for the construction of a small structure of stone rubble that has been described as a mission/fort. The flat lands below, beside a sometimes live stream, were planted to provide crops for later consumption.

During an exploration of the surroundings, an area 8 miles west of the gulf, called *Londó* by the Indians, was chosen as a base camp and provisioning point for further probes into the interior, and noted as a possible mission site. Exploration was not continued because of difficulties in obtaining supplies, the shortage of water, and problems making the site self-sustaining. *San Bruno* was abandoned late in May 1685.

Although *San Bruno* is often referred to as a mission/fort, inspection of the site suggests that the small triangular enclosure was built principally to serve as a fortified storage area where a few men could guard what supplies were left behind and what new materials might be brought from the mainland to provision the main party after their forays into the interior. The scant remnants of *San Bruno* are historically significant because they mark the base for the first crossing of the peninsula by land as well as the first attempted establishment of a mission.

After Kino and Atondo left *San Bruno,* no further land explorations or colonization attempts were undertaken on the peninsula until 1697, when Father Juan María de Salvatierra founded *Misión Nuestra Señora de Loreto,* the first successful and permanent settlement in California.

The Spanish soldier, as illustrated on the cover of the second volume of Noticia de la California *by Padre Miguel Venegas, may have been more typically armored with a leather jacket or "cuera" for service on the hot Baja California frontier.*

San Bruno

This field below the mission/fort site was probably cultivated to help supply food to the expedition. The canyon to the right may have held the livestock.

Loreto Sector Map

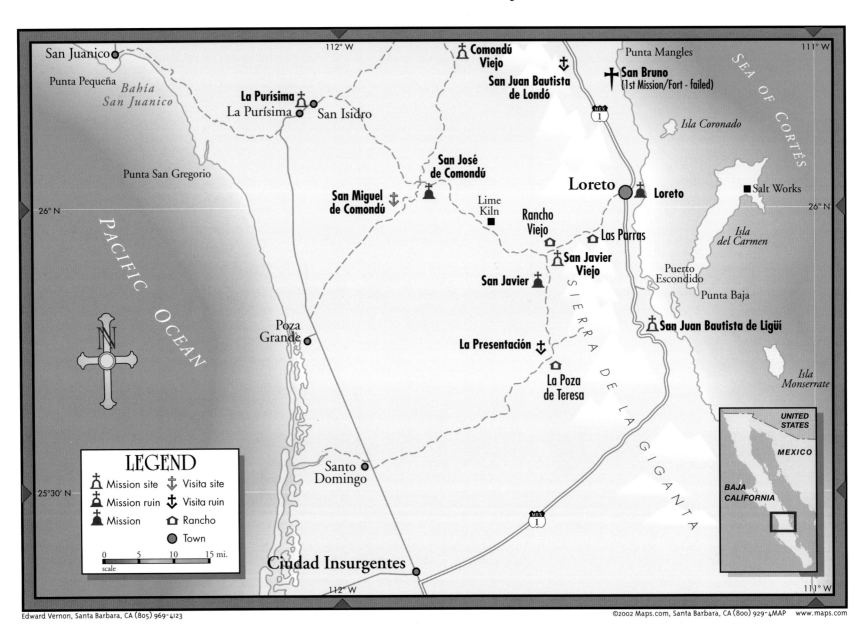

San Juanico

Punta Pequeña

Bahía San Juanico

112° W

Comondú Viejo

Punta Mangles

⚓ San Juan Bautista de Londó

✝ San Bruno
(1st Mission/Fort - failed)

111° W

SEA OF CORTÉS

La Purísima
La Purísima

San Isidro

Isla Coronado

Punta San Gregorio

San José de Comondú

Loreto ● Loreto

■ Salt Works

San Miguel de Comondú ⚓

26° N

Lime Kiln ■

Rancho Viejo

Las Parras

Isla del Carmen

26° N

PACIFIC OCEAN

San Javier Viejo

San Javier

Puerto Escondido

Punta Baja

SIERRA DE LA GIGANTA

⚓ San Juan Bautista de Ligüí

N

Poza Grande

La Presentación ⚓

La Poza de Teresa

Isla Monserrate

UNITED STATES

MEXICO

LEGEND

⛪ Mission site	⚓ Visita site
⛪ Mission ruin	✝ Visita ruin
⛪ Mission	⌂ Rancho
● Town	

Santo Domingo

BAJA CALIFORNIA

25°30′ N

0   5   10   15 mi.

scale

Ciudad Insurgentes

MEX 1

112° W

111° W

Edward Vernon, Santa Barbara, CA (805) 969-4123

1697 – 1829

Misión Nuestra Señora de Loreto de Conchó

FOUNDED BY FATHER JUAN MARÍA DE SALVATIERRA, S.J.

N 26° 00.641' W 110° 20.592'

Misión Nuestra Señora de Loreto de Conchó

The rebuilt church at Loreto stands on the site of the mission church built circa 1704. The tower, completed in 1955, was funded by Father Modesto Sánchez Moyón, who used his lottery winnings for the tower, to restore the church, refurbish the school, and for many other civic improvements. The new stone facade was added after the completion of the tower.

Misión Nuestra Señora de Loreto de Conchó

Father Juan María de Salvatierra landed on the gulf shore of the bay called San Dionisio on October 19, 1697. There, after determining the site suitable, he claimed the land in the name of the King of Spain and on October 25, conducted the ceremonies appropriate to establish the first permanent California mission, *Nuestra Señora de Loreto.*

Still believed to be an island by many, California beckoned the Jesuits as a new and fertile field for evangelization and the saving of souls in a populous land virtually untouched by western civilization.

Salvatierra and Father Eusebio Kino worked together in New Spain to obtain permission to establish missions on the mysterious and fabled peninsula. Kino had, of course, previous experience in California as the religious leader with the short-lived expedition led by Admiral Atondo in 1683, and had a strong desire to return to teach the Catholic faith to the many natives he believed to be receptive to his message. Father Salvatierra, who had become inspector-general of the missions in northwest New Spain, longed to reach the peninsula to continue his work of teaching and conversion.

A bronze bust of Father Salvatierra, decorated with flowers for a local fiesta, stands in the plaza and faces the entry of the mission church he founded.

Misión Nuestra Señora de Loreto de Conchó

On February 5, 1697, Salvatierra obtained permission from the viceroy to embark on the spiritual conquest so important to him and Father Kino. Not only was permission granted but the Jesuits were given authority over both the military and civil officials, an arrangement that had never before been allowed. The Jesuits assumed the power to establish a theocracy, and develop the peninsula and its inhabitants in the manner they deemed best.

This new political structure was granted with one very important proviso—no royal funds were to be used to finance the venture. This meant that all monies required for the new missions were to be raised by the Jesuits, a unique financial situation that resulted in the establishment of the "Pious Fund." Wealthy, devout donors were sought to provide the necessary capital to found, build, provision, and maintain the structures necessary for new missions as they spread throughout the southern part of the peninsula.

Above left: *"The ancient bells of Loreto" were photographed in 1905 by Arthur North. The church tower, said to have been built in 1744, had fallen during the severe 1877 earthquake after years of neglect.*

Left: *The construction of Father Sánchez's tower had just been started when this photo by Neal Harlow was taken at the beginning of 1951. The facade of the church, at that time, appears to be plaster over stone.*

Salvatierra procured two ships to take missionaries and supplies to the new site. As the ships were loading and preparing for departure from Port Yaqui to cross the Sea of Cortés, Father Kino was called back into his area of evangelization in the mountains of the mainland to help quell an uprising by the Indians. Father Salvatierra left port on October 10, 1697, forced to proceed without his friend and co-planner.

The crossing of the gulf was difficult and windy. The *Santa Elvira*, bearing Father Salvatierra, was separated from the second ship, the *El Rosario*. Salvatierra's ship was forced to take refuge in Concepción Bay, 40 miles north of the original target of San Bruno, the site of the failed Atondo-Kino settlement. Several days later the storm abated, and a successful landing was made at San Bruno. However, Father Salvatierra was discouraged from founding his mission there because of the limited water supply.

He eventually sailed to San Dionisio Bay where there was a previously explored, low, mesquite-covered mesa next to an *arroyo* with standing water. *Conchó*, the Indian name for the site, was 20 miles south of San Bruno; there Father Salvatierra and his small party landed to found the first permanent settlement in California.

The boxed and barreled provisions from the ship were placed several hundred yards from the beach in a rectangle to form the walls of a defensive barricade. A tent was erected inside the quadrangle, the adored statue of the Virgin of Loreto carefully placed in the tent, and Salvatierra's first church was dedicated to the Virgin.

The Indians, who were given food to aid in the strenuous work of unloading the ship's stores, began to aggressively demand food and trinkets. The Spaniards then decided to surround the barricade of provisions with a trench backed with thorn bushes and cactus as a defensive and security measure.

It was well that these steps were taken as, after the departure of the *Santa*

The Spanish inscription over the door reads, "The Head and Mother of the Missions of Baja and Alta California." The founding date, 25 October, 1697, is carved into the stone pedestal below the niche.

The choir loft may be seen well elevated over the main entry door. Cedar beams support the flat roof and span the 20-foot-wide nave.

Elvira to fetch another shipload of provisions from the mainland, the Indians began a series of attacks in order to confiscate the food and stores, which the force of 10—six soldiers, three *Yaqui* Indians, and Father Salvatierra—were able to repel. To further raise the spirits of the tiny force, the lost launch *El Rosario* soon appeared bearing reinforcements, additional stores, and farm animals, all contributed by the missions of the mainland. This was to be an often repeated scenario—the needy Baja California missions barely surviving until food and other necessities were brought across the gulf.

In keeping with the original plan to make each mission self-sufficient, water systems, garden fields, corrals, and trails were laboriously constructed. Unfortunately, the dry and rocky terrain surrounding the mission was not able to support the crops and herds necessary to sustain even the small number of people at the mission, and *Loreto* was always dependent on outside sources for the bulk of its food and supplies.

Father Piccolo crossed the gulf on the second provisioning run to join Salvatierra. They soon elected to improve their tenuous foothold by founding a new mission in an area better suited to produce much-needed foodstuffs, and to make their message available to a wider group of natives.

Piccolo led a party of 10 soldiers into the Sierra Giganta, mountains that rise sharply from the narrow plain west of *Loreto,* to find a high plateau called *Viggé* by the Indians, said to have ample perennial water for crops. Here in the spring of 1699 he founded, by the side of a watercourse called *Biaundó, Misión San Francisco Javier de Viggé-Biaundó.*

At Loreto in 1699, a permanent church and service buildings were commenced outside the *presidio* walls. Typical mission construction was employed. Deep, wide trenches were filled with rocks and boulders to above ground level to serve as the foundation for adobe walls. The roof of the structure probably was initially covered with palm thatch, as tile was made later. The church was completed in 1704.

Later, under the supervision of the knowledgeable and energetic Padre Juan de Ugarte, several stone-and-mortar buildings were added to the compound. Paving and roofing tiles were fabricated to finish the new buildings and the church in proper Spanish style.

The small community continued to grow in spite of numerous difficulties and hardships, such as the measles epidemic of 1710 that wiped out one-half of the native population at *Loreto, San Javier,* and *Ligüí.* Food remained the major problem, and the oft-delayed supplies from the mainland forced the small community to the brink of starvation several times during its early life.

Nevertheless, Loreto functioned as the capital and center for many of the activities on the peninsula. Soldiers were garrisoned at the presidio of Loreto to protect all the missions. They also were used to bring back "runaways," and ensure that once initiated into mission life, the natives continued to receive indoctrination into the faith.

The soldiers doubled as craftsmen—as carpenters, stonemasons, blacksmiths, and in other useful trades. A contingent of sailors, at one time as many as 30, lived in the *pueblo* to build, maintain, and sail the small fleet of vessels that were used to transport provisions to Loreto and distribute them to the service ports for the other missions.

During the Jesuit era, *Loreto* was one of the few missions with a substantial mixed population, including civilians, tradesmen, a military contingent, and families. Most of the other missions were limited to a single padre with a servant and a lone soldier to convert, educate, and civilize the Indians.

By 1734, *Loreto*'s growing secular population necessitated larger religious facilities. A stone-and-mortar enlargement of the church was commenced by Father Jaime Bravo in 1740. Bravo's plan was ambitious in scale—the extended building would be over 150 feet long and 20 feet wide. The building, whose basic configuration still stands, was covered by a flat roof of tile and earth over a cedar-beamed ceiling 28 feet above the tile floor. A bell tower was built but its configuration was not recorded.

The beautiful retablo covered with gold leaf stands at the end of the long central aisle of the church, and is adorned with a statue of the Virgin of Loreto.

Misión Nuestra Señora de Loreto de Conchó

A natural cross, with almost human form, stands in the courtyard between the church and museum. It appears to commemorate the 300th year of Loreto's founding, and the base carries the symbol of the Jesuits, the founders of the pueblo and the first California mission.

This church, portions of which are incorporated into the present church, was beautifully decorated inside with an ornate gold-leaf altar plus many valuable religious paintings and statuary, but was described as appearing barn- or warehouse-like from the exterior.

Bravo also built a stone residence, then by far the largest home in Loreto, for himself. That building stood on the southwest corner of the church plaza, and its foundations and those walls still standing after the earthquake of 1877 were used for the residence and store now on the same site.

By 1740, the presidio of Loreto included barracks and housing, storerooms and warehouses, a church, school buildings, homes for the religious staff and visitors, as well as the necessary service buildings, such as carpenter and blacksmith shops. Quarters were also built for the neophytes with separate, secured buildings, as dictated by the padres for the unmarried Indian women. A Spanish *pueblo* had been built on the hostile shores of the thorn- and rock-covered California peninsula.

By the late 1760s, the native population of Loreto was over 400 in addition to the *mestizos*, soldiers, sailors, artisans, and the religious contingent. Several hundred Indians from *rancherías* in the surrounding gulf coast area also came under the mission's charge. Loreto functioned as the base for civil and military authority as well as the religious center of Baja California.

Governor Don Gaspar de Portolá and 15 soldiers arrived from New Spain late in 1767 with orders to expel the Jesuits from the peninsula. The priests were commanded to assemble in Loreto to hear the decree of King Carlos III.

On February 4, 1768, the Jesuits sailed under military guard bound for New Spain and Europe, leaving behind the many missions they had built in the harsh land, and the primitive natives they had so fervently labored to civilize.

The famous Father Junípero Serra and 15 Franciscan priests arrived in *Loreto* late in March of the same year to administer the Jesuit missions. The Franciscans stayed on the peninsula only four years before they moved northward to assume their well-known role in the development of the 21 missions in what is now the state of California.

On May 12, 1773, authorization for Dominican administration arrived in *Loreto,* and soon 27 priests were dispatched throughout the peninsula to replace the Franciscans.

Loreto maintained its position as capital of the Californias until 1776, when Monterey was made capital of both upper and lower California. Loreto then became a regional capital and peninsular headquarters for the missionaries and the military.

A devastating smallpox epidemic swept the peninsula in 1781 and reduced the 162 villagers, counted in 1774, to only 70. Captain Arillaga, arriving in 1785, found the few people surviving desperately short of food and dressed in rags, as no supplies had been received from the mainland in three years.

Loreto must have continued to deteriorate, as during the period of 1790 to 1799, only five births and 10 deaths were recorded in the mission books. An influx of immigrants from the mainland

in 1800 briefly increased Loreto's inhabitants, but the colonists spread throughout the region quickly, and the population continued to decline.

By 1829, the pueblo lost its status as the regional capital, and this date also marks the end of Loreto's mission era as no missionary or Indians remained at the crumbling mission compound. By 1850, there were no Indians on the peninsula south of *Santa Gertrudis.* A visitor in 1854 said Loreto was virtually in ruins.

Bravo's church, commenced in 1740, still stands although it is often repaired. It has survived hurricanes, floods, and violent earthquakes, including the fearsome quake in 1877 that produced strong aftershocks for six weeks. The villagers fled to the mountains in terror, but eventually returned to rebuild their homes and restore their precious church.

Loreto still maintains a bit of its mission pueblo charm but is fast becoming a tourist destination, as evidenced by cruise boat visits, exclusive hotels, and resorts. Father Salvatierra certainly would be amazed by the changes in the village he created so many years ago.

The mother and child, photographed by North in 1905, are sitting in front of the altar of the side chapel. The Virgin of Loreto is the same statue brought by Father Salvatierra from Spain and first placed in the temporary tent church in 1697.

Misión Nuestra Señora de Loreto de Conchó

Northwest of town on the side of a shallow arroyo, this well-like kiln was carved into a solid conglomerate rock ledge about 6 feet high. Alternate layers of sticks and limestone were added from the 3-foot-diameter top opening. The stack was then fired to change the stone into "cal," which when finely ground and mixed with sand and water, formed mortar or plaster. At the base of the "horno," a small semicircular opening gave access to the fired stone.

1699 – 1817

Misión San Francisco Javier
de Viggé-Biaundó

FOUNDED BY FATHER FRANCISCO MARÍA PICCOLO, S.J.

N 25° 51.663'   W 111° 32.627'

Misión San Francisco Javier de Viggé-Biaundó

The morning sun illuminates the recently paved plaza in front of the beautiful old stone church.

Misión San Francisco Javier de Viggé-Biaundó

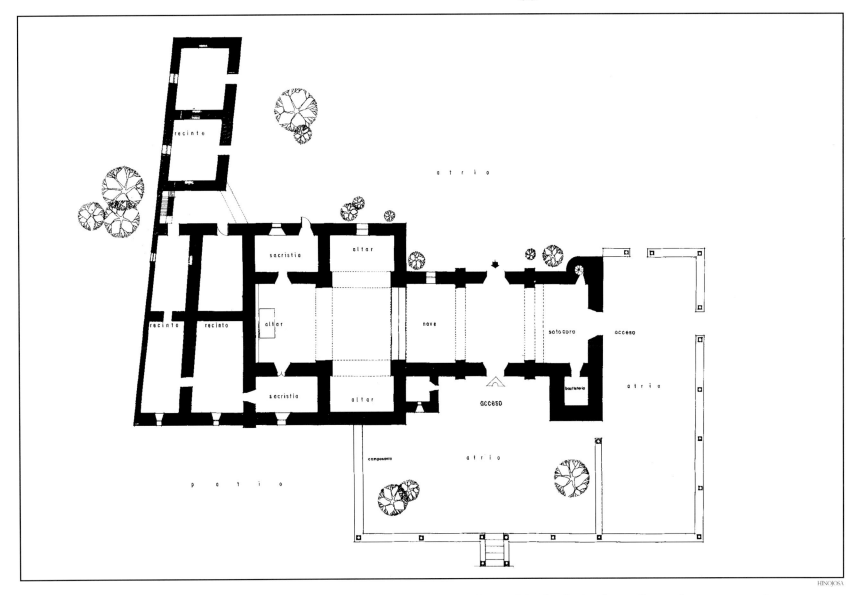

The cruciform north-facing church includes outbuildings and patios, and the burial ground lies beside the altar wall near the east entry to the nave.

Misión San Francisco Javier de Viggé-Biaundó

San Javier Viejo, the first site of the mission, is high in the Sierra Giganta near the present *Rancho Viejo*, 20 miles south of Loreto and 5 miles north of the stone church at the final site. Little is left of the structures that were built here by Father Piccolo in 1699 to establish *Misión San Francisco Javier*. A few stones mark the foundations of a 12 by 20-foot chapel and the two other adobe buildings that Piccolo erected.

As the site is on the edge of a field that has often been cultivated, the remnants have been nearly obliterated. However, a substantial dam of rock and mortar and an irrigation system one-half mile east of the building site are in amazingly good condition. This location, at the spring called *Biaundó* by the *Cochimí*, was deserted by Father Piccolo and his few soldiers in 1701 because of a threatened Indian revolt.

An acequia leads downstream from the dam along the arroyo bank, and is used today to route plastic water pipe to gardens below.

The dam at the first site, viewed from the downstream side, has withstood the occasional Baja California downpour and torrential flooding for more than three centuries.

The first mission stood on this flat— only a few foundation stones remain.

Misión San Francisco Javier de Viggé-Biaundó

The remarkable Juan de Ugarte reestablished the deserted mission in 1702, and struggled with the lack of water and exposure to the wind at the original site for some years. A better watered location, San Pablo, was selected 5 miles downstream where the *arroyo* is sheltered by high lava canyon walls. Here Ugarte built several reservoirs and irrigation systems to expand the area's food-producing capability; as it was not possible to grow sufficient food at Loreto to feed the population, products from the *sierra* farms were necessary for the survival of the early missions. An abundance of fruit and vegetables was grown, including beans, citrus, dates, sugarcane, and grapes. Cotton was also farmed, and sheep were raised for meat and wool. The natives were taught to weave, and both cotton and woolen fabrics were produced. Ugarte also had the distinction of making the first wine in California from the grapes grown at *San Javier,* in about 1710.

Neal Harlow and friend ride into San Javier on muleback in 1951.

The entry monument has stood facing the church for more than two centuries.

Misión San Francisco Javier de Viggé-Biaundó

A small graveyard lies between the tower and the low wall on the east side of the church.

The west side features an intricately detailed door and window.

Father Juan de Ugarte was certainly one of the most important and creative missionaries on the peninsula. He not only revived *San Javier Viejo,* but he constructed the first stone buildings at the present site, made dams and aqueducts, and established gardens at *San Miguel* in the arroyo 20 miles to the north that would soon be known as *Comondú.* He also logged the mountains west of *Mulegé* to provide the timber to build *El Triunfo de la Cruz,* the first ship built in California. In addition to his material accomplishments and great physical strength, he was an outstanding spiritual leader, a stirring preacher and priest, and a most prodigious savior of souls. He died on December 28, 1730, at *Misión San Javier.*

Misión San Francisco Javier de Viggé-Biaundó

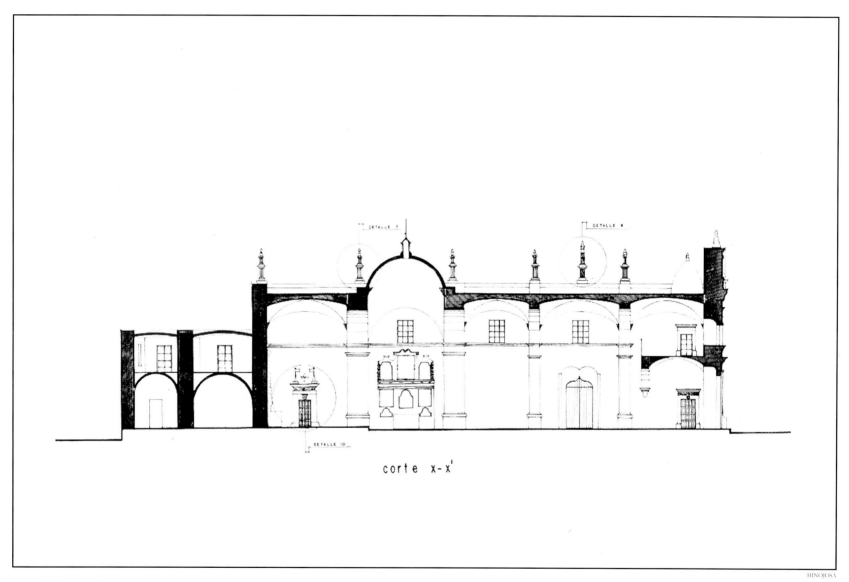

The complex construction of the chapel, as well as the placement of the side altar and the choir loft, is clearly shown in this longitudinal cross-section.

Misión San Francisco Javier de Viggé-Biaundó

The jewel of the Baja California mission churches, which now stands at San Javier, was commenced in 1744 by Father Miguel del Barco and completed in 1758. This remarkable structure used quarried stone set with mortar from cement made of local limestone. A kiln (El Horno) located 10 miles distant, midway between missions *San Javier* and *Comondú*, may have been used to fire the limestone as part of the cement-making process. The labor involved in mining the limestone, transporting the ore to the kiln, gathering and cutting trees and sticks for fuel, then firing the stone to enable it to be ground into cement, is almost beyond comprehension. After this laborious process, the cement had to be transported to the building site, where it was mixed with sand and water to make mortar. Another kiln, located at

Far right: *This detailed carved stone facade surrounds the window venting the choir loft and is located directly over the main entry.*

Right: *A stone cross placed over the east entry is silhouetted against the deep-set window.*

Rancho El Horno, only a few miles upstream from the mission, may have been the first oven used to manufacture the precious cement. In fact, the kiln between *San Javier* and *Comondú,* generally credited with providing the fired limestone for both missions, could have been built near the end of the construction era. The inside shows very little evidence of use (soot and glazing), and therefore kilns closer to each of the sites were probably the sources of cement for most of the mortar.

Stone for the mission walls must have been quarried and trimmed to accurate rectangular blocks in a nearby canyon. A skilled stonemason was imported from the mainland to supervise and train the Indians to build the high mission walls and construct the vaulted roof of the nave. The lofty, domed bell tower looks over the deep valley, and the cornice of the main structure is lined with decoratively carved stone cone-shaped *pináculos.*

Above: *The grille in front of the circular stairway to the bell tower and roof must have been replaced many times. However, it is probably typical of the original type of door.*

Left: *The choir loft and entry are viewed from the altar area. Can you imagine a native choir singing melodies learned from the padres during mass?*

Misión San Francisco Javier de Viggé-Biaundó

The body of the church is formed in the shape of a cross, with the main altar directly in front of the barrel-vaulted nave and the two side altars placed in the arms of the cross. The focal point of the impressive cruciform church is the beautiful *retablo* that covers the entire wall behind the central altar in the vaulted nave.

This intricately carved altarpiece features a polychrome statue of Saint Xavier surrounded by eight oil paintings from the 18th century. The enormous retablo, covered in gold leaf, was created in New Spain, separated into pieces, shipped across the gulf, then carried in 32 crates on the backs of pack animals up the steep torturous trail from Loreto. The retablo

Far left: *The beautiful altarpiece featuring Saint Xavier was completely refurbished in 1999, just prior to the celebration of the mission's 300th birthday.*

Left: *In 1999, the paintings in the side altars were cleaned and the altars repaired and reconstructed.*

Near right: *The precious robes are stored in the sacristy.*

Middle right: *A statue of Mary is displayed in a side altar.*

Far right: *Saint Xavier makes a striking centerpiece for the main retablo.*

Misión San Francisco Javier de Viggé-Biaundó

was completely restored in 1999 and viewing it, as well as the beautiful church and the small village, is well worth the 23-mile, steep twisting drive from Loreto.

A smaller but similar gilded retablo stands in each of the two side altars. Ceremonial robes, perhaps from the 18th century, are kept in a glass-fronted case in the sacristy behind the altars. The large choir loft, served by a spiral stone staircase, overlooks the nave, and three altars are decorated with statues and many other fine pieces of religious artwork.

Misión San Francisco Javier de Viggé-Biaundó

Before the Indians were ravaged and depleted by disease in the early days of the mission, several thousand must have lived in the sierra. *Misión San Javier* included six or seven visiting stations scattered over many miles of the Sierra Giganta to serve the large number of indigenous inhabitants.

In the 1768 inventory, at a time when many of the other missions' populations had decreased by a factor of 10, 480 Christians were counted at *Misión San Javier*. By 1800, that number had decreased to 111, and in 1817 the mission was deserted, as virtually no natives had survived.

Stone roof drains extend like cannons from the sturdy wall of the building that adjoins the church.

This side entry displays a decorative lintel and a delicate carved grille.

Carving on a door casing shows the care and skill exerted to embellish the church.

Misión San Francisco Javier de Viggé-Biaundó

The mission is in wonderful condition, thanks to continued maintenance and restoration work by the National Institute of History and Anthropology (INAH), and it still serves the local village and surrounding ranching community when a padre is available for mass. What a pleasure it is to see this historic monument, which remains virtually unchanged after 250 years in its remote and rugged, high mountain setting!

Right: *One of the great sights in Baja California is the first view of the tower of San Javier peeking through the palms in the deep canyon.*

Below: *The dam upstream from the mission is often dry, but when filled provides water to the fields surrounding the mission, as it did in Ugarte's day.*

Misión San Francisco Javier de Viggé-Biaundó

El Horno, "the oven," was used to fire limestone in the laborious but very necessary mortar-making process. This well-preserved kiln stands in the sierra halfway between San Javier and Comondú.

1699 – 1750

Visita San Juan Bautista de Londó

FOUNDED BY FATHERS JUAN MARÍA SALVATIERRA, S.J.
& FRANCISCO MARÍA PICCOLO, S.J.

N 26º 13.501' W 111º 28.405'

Visita San Juan Bautista de Londó

This single wall stands amid the stone rubble and remnants of Visita San Juan Bautista de Londó. The well-pointed stonework indicates the recent restoration when the disintegrating mortar was partially removed and replaced with fresh grout. A small cemetery close by is the only other reminder of the padres' attempt to Christianize and bring western civilization to the Cochimí natives.

VERNON, 1998

34

Visita San Juan Bautista de Londó

In 1699, close friends Fathers Juan María de Salvatierra and Francisco María Piccolo established a visiting station 20 miles north of *Loreto* at a *Cochimí ranchería* called *Londó*. This site, 8 miles west of the Sea of Cortés, was known by the Spanish, as it had been used as a provisioning camp in 1683 for the Kino-Atondo expedition.

The *visita* is located next to a few ranch houses on a small flat above a mostly dry creek bed, in a broad watercourse that slopes from the Sierra Giganta to the gulf. San Bruno Bay, at the mouth of the same *arroyo*, was the expedition's landing point, and a nearby hill still carries the rock outline of the fortification built in 1683.

In 1705, the construction of a permanent stone structure was undertaken at *Londó* by Father Salvatierra, and the ruins of his well-detailed small chapel still stand today. A cemetery with rock-covered graves adjoins the chapel ruins, as well as several thatch houses, corrals, and pig pens. Huge cardón cacti are scattered about the west side of the site.

HARLOW, 1945

The picture above shows that not only was the door at the far end of the building intact in 1945, but far more of the vaulted ceiling was in place than currently.

This detail illustrates the fine stone carving that decorates the junction of the side walls with the vaulted roof.

Visita San Juan Bautista de Londó

Above: *Detail of the carved trim over the now-fallen doorway.*

Left: *The window in the single standing wall is missing a section of dental molding and some of the stones above.*

HARLOW, 1945

The south door of the building was intact when this photo was taken over 55 years ago. Note the fine detailing carved into the door lintel and the nicely fitted blocks forming the door jambs. This door and the wall above it no longer stand.

Even though the building is small, 16 by 40 feet, and was to be used only as a visiting station, great care was taken in adorning it with fine detailing in the form of dental molding at wall-top height and ornate carving around the door and window. Construction was of stone, much of it laboriously shaped into blocks to make more regular walls and laid in cement mortar to insure a strong and lasting structure.

A number of large flat fields bordered by tall date palms are scattered about ruins near dry gullies that sometimes carry water. The fields obviously have been cultivated in the past but are now pitifully dusty and arid.

Visita San Juan Bautista de Londó

Although a large Indian population had been able to sustain itself at this ranchería site using traditional hunting and gathering skills, the mission farming/ranching lifestyle did not provide the food necessary to feed the natives. Supplemental food, imported from the mainland, was always required for the Indians who chose to remain there.

A 1708 smallpox epidemic that also ravaged the missions *Loreto* and *Comondú* wiped out a large portion of the natives, and by 1750 the *Londó* Indian population had so diminished that the few remaining neophytes were permanently transferred to *Misión San José de Comondú,* and *Londó* was delegated for use as a way station and abandoned as a visita.

Because it is so desolate and lonely, it is hard to imagine this place first as the encampment of the Kino-Atondo expedition, with a troop of leather-jacketed soldiers, armored horses, and pack animals preparing to cross the almost impenetrable Sierra Giganta, and then as the center for activities that were part of life at the visiting station.

Above right: *Even though this field is perfectly flat and level and was obviously created for farming, it is surprising that enough water was ever available to grow crops. A water system must have provided for irrigation and cultivation in at least some of the 50 years that the site was occupied.*

Right: *Goats and pigs seem to provide the livelihood of the several families that live in these stick-and-thatch houses a few hundred feet from the visita.*

Visita San Juan Bautista de Londó

The Sierra Giganta rise sharply in the background. The ruins of Londó stand amid the cactus and palms in the center. The brown cleared flat, to the left center, marks a dry field that may have been cultivated in mission days.

1705 – 1721

Misión San Juan Bautista de Ligüí

FOUNDED BY FATHER PEDRO DE UGARTE, S.J.

N 25º 44.334'   W 111º 15.874'

The Sierra Giganta forms an imposing barrier when looking westward from the mission site.

Misión San Juan Bautista de Ligüí

Father Pedro de Ugarte, in 1705, founded *Misión San Juan Bautista de Ligüí*, later called *Malibat,* as instructed by Father Juan María de Salvatierra. The original purpose of the mission was to Christianize the *Monquí* and *Cochimí* Indians who populated this gulfside area 20 miles south of Loreto. The site chosen was very poor as there was little land for agriculture, no dependable water and, worst of all, the mission was placed dangerously close to a watercourse between the precipitous slopes of the Sierra Giganta and the gulf.

It is not hard to imagine the fast-moving wall of water that must rush down the rocky arroyo bed below during the downpour of the occasional hurricane. The rock and mortar fragments, on the right and below, are remnants from the mission's foundation. The building's walls were of adobe, as the short life of the mission did not allow time to build a permanent stone structure.

Misión San Juan Bautista de Ligüí

Occasionally torrential floods poured down the shallow *arroyo* next to the mission, which eventually led to its nearly total obliteration. Locally it is said that substantial foundation ruins were in place until 1973, when building of the nearby paved highway caused serious erosion, and most remnants were washed away during a hurricane later in the year.

Not only was the site tenuous on a bench only a little above the arroyo bed, but aggressive *Pericú* Indians from the offshore islands made frequent raids on the mission and the *rancherías* of the mission Indians. To add to the many problems at this location, the annual gift funding necessary for the operation of the mission was lost because of the bankruptcy of the mission's benefactor, Juan Bautista López, a wealthy Mexican landowner.

The final priest at *Misión Ligüí*, Father Clemente Guillén, closed the mission in 1721 and moved the faithful Indians 50 miles south to a perennial spring at a gulfside site called *Apaté* to found *Misión Nuestra Señora de los Dolores.*

Mathes' 1972 photo of the ruins before the 1973 floods, which undercut and washed away most of the foundations abetted by the construction of the peninsular highway.

Misión San Juan Bautista de Ligüí

The only remnants at *Misión Ligüí* are several foundation sections of river rock bound with mortar. These remains, on a mesquite-covered knoll only a few feet above the arroyo bed, are located about midway between the highway and the gulf, one-quarter mile east of the school and the tiny village of *Ligüí*.

It is likely that future runoff from a typical violent Baja California storm will eventually erase all physical signs of this unfortunate and vulnerable site.

The view looking southeast toward the gulf from the mission site is ruggedly beautiful, but shows the dry sandy terrain that even hard work and tremendous faith could not overcome.

Misión San Juan Bautista de Ligüí

An artist in Spain made this drawing of the South Cape natives from descriptions supplied by the peninsula padres.

1705 – 1828

Misión Santa Rosalía de Mulegé

FOUNDED BY FATHER JUAN MANUEL DE BASALDÚA, S.J.

N 26° 53.227' W 111° 59.170'

Misión Santa Rosalía de Mulegé

TOM PLOCH, 1999

The Jesuits started building this stone church in 1766. Many additions and refurbishments have since been made.

Misión Santa Rosalía de Mulegé

Father Salvatierra in 1703 initiated two expeditions from Loreto, one up and the other down the coast, to expand the area of the missionaries' influence to the natives who lived along the gulf. New missions were established at Indian *rancherías* in *Mulegé*, 60 miles north, and at *Ligüí,* 20 miles south of Loreto. These additions to the existing missions at Loreto and San Javier increased the number of Jesuit sites to four.

The estuary at *Mulegé* had been found by accident one year earlier, when a provisioning ship from the mainland, bound for Loreto, had been blown off course during a storm. It had taken refuge afforded by the cliffs surrounding the wide mouth of the only perennial river on the gulf side of the peninsula.

As an overland expedition had been unable to penetrate the rugged terrain to reach the site, Fathers Francisco María Piccolo and Juan Basaldúa, in August 1703, organized a seaborne party from Loreto on the mission launch to the beautiful palm-lined inlet at *Mulegé*. Three miles inland, they found ample water and land for mission buildings and crops.

The building to the left of the tower is the parish hall, and is used for many civic functions. The thick stone walls and vaulted roof are of materials similar to those used in the church, but the date of construction may have been later.

An external entry to the choir loft is served by the steep stairway.

The rear of the parish hall is either being repaired or remodeled. This process has been repeated many times in the nearly 250 years of life of the mission.

Father Basaldúa returned to *Loreto* to plan for the provisioning of the new mission. In November 1705, leading a pack train of supplies and a squad of soldiers, he established *Misión Santa Rosalía de Mulegé* in the green and fertile land populated by peaceful and receptive Indians. Basaldúa soon built an adobe church and living quarters as well as commenced a typical mission irrigation system.

A terrible hurricane in 1717 devastated the missions at Loreto and San Javier, where it was reported that the adobe churches and houses were washed away. At *Mulegé,* the life-sustaining agricultural fields were scoured by the floods, leaving only barren rocky surfaces. Little is written about the progress of the mission until 1766, when the construction of a stone church was started by Father Escalante at what probably

Misión Santa Rosalía de Mulegé

was a new and safer site chosen after the hurricane, high on the bluff overlooking the deep, water-filled inlet.

On the assumption of the responsibility for all of the Baja California missions by the Franciscans in 1768, Father Serra assigned *Mulegé* and its "three hundred native Christians" to the charge of Father Juan Gastón. The disruption caused by the departure of the Jesuits, the short tenure of the Franciscans, and the incompetent military administration in the absence of the missionaries caused serious deterioration of the missions and their Indians.

By 1770, *Misión Santa Rosalía de Mulegé* was virtually deserted, and the Dominicans began rebuilding. In 1783, only 20 families with a total of 75 people occupied the mission and its lands. In 1794, a kitchen was built, and four years later, six adobe, flat earthen-roofed dwellings were added for the Indians. By 1800, the native population living at the mission was counted at 90.

However, the fortunes of the mission continued to decline, as shown by a report on the ability of certain missions to pay a 25-peso tax. Ramón López, soon to be the Dominican president, stated that, "Nothing can be realistically expected from the Missions of Mulegé, Comondú and San Javier,

The solemn main entry leads beneath the choir loft into the cool and dim interior.

all of which are on their last breaths." In 1828, *Misión Santa Rosalía de Mulegé* was rapidly deteriorating, and the scant and declining population made abandonment necessary.

After the mission era, an interesting historical footnote involved *Mulegé* because of its brief role in the Mexican-American war. United States forces had occupied La Paz to prevent Baja California Mexican forces from joining the resistance to the invasion. American assaults were made at San José del Cabo and *Mulegé,* where a one-day skirmish erupted. On October 3, 1847, American sailors aboard the sloop-of-war U.S.S. *Dale* attacked *Mulegé* with a force of 47 men. They skirmished with the local Mexican loyalists in the *arroyo* and on the outskirts of the village. Perhaps the deserted mission was used as a vantage point by the Mexican soldiers.

The deepset window that allows light to penetrate the shadowy interior reveals the thick, sturdy stone walls of the chapel.

Misión Santa Rosalía de Mulegé

The altar has been recently refurbished and blends nicely with the simple interior of the beautifully kept church.

From the interior, the choir loft over the entry may be viewed. Access to the loft is by an exterior stairway.

After the one-day battle, the American forces withdrew, feeling "that the chastisement inflicted on the people of *Mulegé* will effectually deter them from any further measures of hostility towards Americans in California." The defenders felt that the Americans had abandoned the battle after being given "exemplary punishment" by the Mexicans as they fought for their native land. All battles should end so well—with both sides feeling victorious and few, if any, casualties.

The mission across the arroyo from the *pueblo* of *Mulegé* overlooking the battlefield has had many restorations and is in excellent condition. It now serves as a parish church and community center, a tourist attraction, and an imposing reminder of the mission days in Baja California.

Misión Santa Rosalía de Mulegé

PLOCH, 1999

The walkway around the buildings affords sweeping views of the inlet from the gulf and the village on the opposite side of the canyon.

1708 – 1827

Misión San José de Comondú

FOUNDED BY FATHER JULIÁN DE MAYORGA, S.J.

N 26º 03.618′   W 111º 49.315′

Misión San José de Comondú

A computer reconstruction of the church and chapel as they were in the late 1700s.

Misión San José de Comondú

Left: The first site – 1708

Established in a high canyon 30 miles northwest of Loreto, these remaining foundations of the chapel mark the area now called "Comondú Viejo."

Below: The second site – 1736

Nothing is left of the mission and visita at San Miguel except a few walls and foundations that must have been made from remnants of the fallen mission.

Above: The third site – 1737

The chapel, one of two standing structures, as well as many foundations and partial walls, mark the final mission location.

Misión San José de Comondú – Comondú Viejo

Founded in 1708 by Father Julián de Mayorga at a place called *Comondú* by the *Cochimí,* the first site of *Misión San José de Comondú* is still plainly identifiable. A stone foundation outlines an area 20 by 70 feet that must have been the chapel. Adjacent are the stone ruins of a building 20 by 40 feet that was probably the home of Father Mayorga. Even though the walls of this structure were laid without mortar, wall sections of up to 6 feet in height still stand.

Two *pilas,* one 300 yards upstream from the chapel and the other about one mile down the *arroyo,* are part of an irrigation system that included many thousands of feet of rock-lined *acequias.* In spite of these storage and distribution efforts, there simply was not enough water to raise crops and provide for the indigenous population by European farming methods.

The tenuous first site 30 miles northwest of Loreto, in a shallow canyon choked with thick cactus and undergrowth, is dusty and dry as well as dark and foreboding. The only activity is the herding of cattle and goats. A small thatched house near the mission ruins provides shelter for the ranchers.

In 1710, a smallpox epidemic killed half of *Comondú's* converts and also ravaged *Loreto* and *San Javier.* Retaining its original name and its Indians, *Misión Comondú* was moved in 1736 to *Visita San Miguel,* 30 miles southwest. Considering the many problems, it is surprising the move was not made earlier.

Left: *These foundation ruins clearly outline the chapel footprint.*

Above: *Wall segments of the priests' casa stand next to the chapel.*

Right: *Pancho Bareño, our guide, points to the stone-and-mortar wall of the pila.*

Misión San José de Comondú – San Miguel

The site of the picturesque colonial village named San Miguel was discovered by Fathers Salvatierra and Ugarte in 1707. They met by chance in the beautiful canyon while each was leading a separate expedition through the *sierra* looking for possible mission sites. Because of its rich soil, water, and many Indian *rancherías,* Father Juan Ugarte seven years later established a *visita* and farm there to supply *Misión San Javier,* and named it *San Miguel.*

Misión San José de Comondú and its neophytes were moved to *San Miguel* in 1736 to take advantage of its favorable farming conditions. There is no indication of the size or number of buildings at what was an important visiting station and, for a short time, a mission. There must have been a church, as well as several buildings to hold stores and serve as hous-

ing for the priests, workers, and soldiers. Throughout the *pueblo,* there are remnants of the mission. Well-cut stone, probably from fallen mission structures, has been used to make garden walls, porch steps, and sections of the walls of village homes and outbuildings.

Few people now live in the village and many of the adobe buildings on the plaza are abandoned. However, the gardens still yield grapes, olives, dates, and citrus. The area retains a strong feeling of the past, and life moves at a languid pace with a charming tranquillity.

In 1737, *Misión San José de Comondú* made its third and final move 2 miles upstream to the location of a visita called *San Ignacio.* After this move the prior sites, *San Miguel* and *Comondú Viejo,* continued to serve as visiting stations.

The stone wall above is typical of many structures made of mission remnants. The weathered adobe buildings, shown to the left, face the nearly deserted village plaza.

Misión San José de Comondú

SIMONS, 1997

The old stone chapel at the final site of Misión San José de Comondú.

58

Misión San José de Comondú

At its new site, adobe structures were erected to reestablish *Misión San José de Comondú*. The buildings were constructed next to a perennial stream amid the lush greenery of a palm-lined arroyo, to later be replaced by a large stone complex commenced in 1750 by Father Franz Inama. The church, one side of a large quadrangle, was the largest and perhaps most beautifully decorated church in Baja California.

The mission locale was extensively developed, and the canyon bottom from the new location downstream to San Miguel served as a prolific and much-needed mission garden. That area still yields an abundance of fruit and vegetables.

Although the main church has fallen, a simple stone chapel, originally attached to the side of the altar of the grand church, still stands. This lovely chapel with thick stone walls, a vaulted brick roof, ruined wall segments, a variety of artifacts, a square masonry building later used as a jail, and foundation remnants scattered among the palms surrounding the chapel are all that have survived the 250 years since the mission was constructed.

The chapel, which abutted the altar end of the main structure, had an interior wall to divide it into a chapel and a sacristy. That wall was removed during the 1973 renovation, which included building a new facade with the original mission rubble.

Neal Harlow's 1951 photo shows the remnants of the wall behind the altar of the three-nave church and the bricked-up face of the chapel. The 1936 demolition of the church ruins made room for a school that now too has been demolished.

Misión San José de Comondú

This exterior detail shows the fine stonework surrounding the window as well as the ornate wooden grill that shields the opening.

The old stone church, which measured 50 by 145 feet, had three barrel-vaulted naves nearly 30 feet high, each with an altar at the end. The chapel, attached near the altar in an ell configuration, is 25 feet wide and 75 feet in length.

The front of the church, of rectangular-cut stone, included an ornate entry with carved stone ornamentation featuring a replica of the coat of arms of the aristocratic and titled Villapuente family, the wealthy donors who funded the church. A large cobblestone plaza covered the ground directly in front of the church steps.

The rear corner of the chapel is viewed across what was the front courtyard. The ruins to the right may be those of the building added in 1798.

A large window directly over the main entry door opened into the choir loft. Two niches, one on each side of the window, were outlined by carved stone frames and probably held religious statuary. The church bells hung on a wooden framework next to the main entry.

Opposing sides of the church included impressive doorways flanked by square ornamental towers capped with domes, and topped with stone cups holding carved stone flames. The interior must have been very beautiful, with the barrel-vaulted ceilings supported at their junctions by what North called "eight Grecian pillars, each a metre in diameter, placed [in two rows of] four on either side of the main aisle…"

Above: *Skillful stonework was employed to carve the cross decorating the keystone and fashion the casing surrounding the door serving the cross aisle of the chapel.*

Left: *The ruins directly behind the chapel are said by the locals to be the remnants of the kitchen. This building was in all probability the 1798 addition described as being "six by nineteen varas" (16 by 51 feet). As the windows of the building were wider outside than inside, the opposite of the chapel windows, it must have been constructed at a different time.*

Misión San José de Comondú

The exterior doorway led from the northern perimeter of the mission, through a housing wing, into the garden enclosed by the chapel, the kitchen, and rooms.

Above: *A carved stone flame graced each of the four towers.*

Below: *A stone ornament, now an altar support, stood on the cornice between each pair of towers.*

The window viewed across the altar reveals the thick (over 3 feet) stone walls.

The bell on the left of the three bells now displayed in the chapel is dated 1697.

Misión San José de Comondú

An inventory, taken in 1768 in anticipation of part of the mission's possessions being requisitioned for a new mission to be established by Father Junípero Serra in San Diego, included the following:

Carved polychrome images, numerous paintings
Many religious articles of silver and gold
A well-equipped kitchen
China, silver, and crystal for household use
Surgical instruments and barber's tools
A variety of blacksmith's and carpenter's tools
Cattle, sheep, and goats
Stores of wine, grains, and foodstuffs

The compound included a courtyard, rooms for the priest with a large library, quarters for soldiers and visiting priests, as well as many other rooms opening to the garden. A jail, blacksmith shop, an enclosed and irrigated garden with a large fountain, and a walled cemetery were also part of this ambitious and extensive development.

Not only is the size and craftsmanship of the mission amazing but, considering that the neophyte population of more than 300 in 1740 had declined to "eighty souls" in 1768, it is remarkable that such an ambitious building project was possible to continue during this era of disease and a rapidly declining population. By 1800, only 28 Indians remained; the mission was abandoned in 1827.

Above right: *The ruins of the blacksmith shop are now overgrown with vines and shrubs.*

Right: *The stone jail is in excellent condition and could still serve as a secure prison.*

Misión San José de Comondú

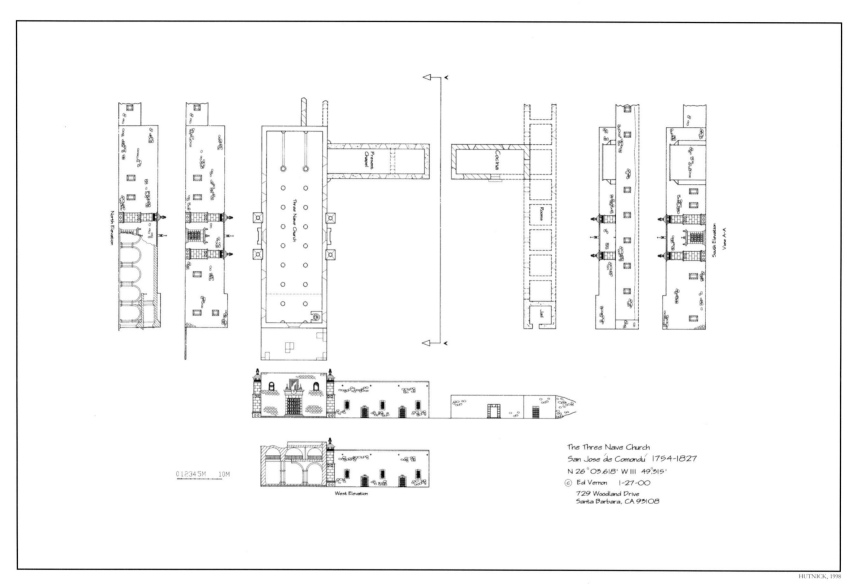

The Three Nave Church
San Jose de Comondú 1754-1827
N 26°03.618' W 111 49.315'
© Ed Vernon 1-27-00
729 Woodland Drive
Santa Barbara, CA 93108

0 1 2 3 4 5M 10M

These elevations and foundation plans were derived from old photographs, site location of foundation remnants, and oral history from local residents.

Misión San José de Comondú

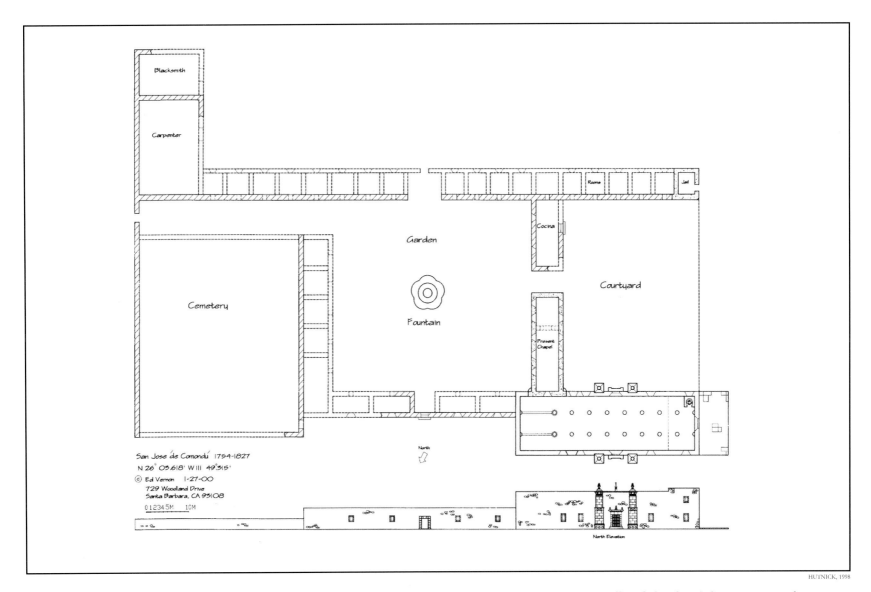

Blacksmith

Carpenter

Rooms

Jail

Cocina

Garden

Courtyard

Cemetery

Fountain

Present Chapel

North

San Jose de Comondú 1754-1827

N 26° 03.618' W III 49°.315'

© Ed Vernon 1-27-00

729 Woodland Drive
Santa Barbara, CA 93108

0 1 2 3 4 5 M   10M

North Elevation

Only the chapel is still intact, but stone foundations and partial walls supplemented with sharp memories allowed the plot of the mission complex.

Misión San José de Comondú

A computer reconstruction of the view from the courtyard of the south-facing side door to the three-nave church.

Misión San José de Comondú

Left: *The doorway and twin towers were modeled from North's 1905 photograph. An identical facade graced the opposite side of the church.*

Right: *The door to the cross aisle has been obstructed to prevent access to the hazardous interior. The carved stone flames that stood on top of the towers are now displayed in the chapel, as is the decorative monument between the towers. Several of the stone "pans" that appear in the midsection of the towers and other remnants of artistically crafted stone ornamentation are found in the mission gardens. In spite of its deterioration, the beauty of this facade was quite apparent when photographed.*

ARTHUR NORTH

Misión San José de Comondú

The north side of the church with attached living quarters as it must have appeared circa 1800, as reconstructed on the computer.

Misión San José de Comondú

Right: *Two horsemen ride by the crumbling north wall of the mission. The source of the photograph is unknown—it was probably taken a few years later than the photo below. The towers flank the side entry to the cross aisle.*

Left: *Arthur North took this photo in 1905 while standing on the wall behind the central altar. The rectangular opening under the roof arch at the far end of the building provided light and ventilation to the choir loft. Note the special configuration of the column in the foreground, which was the column nearest the altar.*

A computer reconstruction shows the west facade before the destruction of the church, with the main entry portal, niches for statuary, and the choir loft window.

The carved shield over the west-facing main entry is a replica of the coat of arms of the titled Villapuente family who financed the building of the mission. The opening over the main door allowed light and air to enter the choir loft. The building extending to the right of the facade is the presently standing chapel that abutted the main church next to the altar area. As the door that now exists in the chapel, located just to the left of the window, does not appear in this photo, it must have been added during the 1973 refurbishment. The source of this photo is unknown but it was probably taken about 1905.

Misión San José de Comondú

This beautiful canyon, which slopes to the Pacific, is the home of descendants of mission soldiers, artisans, and later immigrants from New Spain. The crops that are raised here still sustain the people of San Miguel and San José in a peaceful manner that remains unchanged after several centuries.

1720 – 1822

Misión La Purísima Concepción
de María de Cadegomó

FOUNDED BY FATHER NICOLÁS TAMARAL, S.J.

N 26° 11.426'   W 112° 04.377'

Misión La Purísima Concepción de María de Cadegomó

NORTH, 1905

Mass and other ceremonies were still held at the old church of Misión La Purísima in 1905 in spite of the poor condition of the building.

In 1720, *Misión La Purísima* was founded in Arroyo San Gregorio, a broad canyon 60 miles west of Loreto that slopes to the Pacific Ocean. The area had been noted as a potential mission site by Father Piccolo during his 1712 trip to explore and to initiate religious training for the *Cochimí* Indians. Undoubtedly the numerous Indian *rancherías* there had been recorded by the Kino-Atondo party during their winter 1684–1685 exploratory crossing of the peninsula.

Father Nicolás Tamaral, a young Spanish Jesuit newly arrived in Baja California, was appointed in 1717 to found the mission. A tremendous hurricane, which nearly demolished all of the adobe structures in the lower half of the peninsula, delayed the founding until 1720. Permanent buildings were commenced in 1722 when funding was obtained from the Marquis de Villapuente, a nobleman who was also the donor who enabled the building of the three-nave church at *Comondú*.

74

Misión La Purísima Concepción de María de Cadegomó

By 1735, the mission had been moved to a new location about 20 miles south, called *Cadegomó* by the *Cochimí*. This was its final site—a lush, well-watered, and lava-cliff-lined *arroyo* now called *La Purísima*. According to a report by visitador-general Echeverría, it was one of the most populous and productive of the Jesuit missions in Baja California.

Englehardt states that the church at *La Purísima* in 1793 was of adobe and measured 25 by 6½ *varas* (80 by 20 feet). A house and a library for the priest were part of the complex. The precise location of those buildings is not known—however, they were probably very close to the stone church at the final location photographed by North in 1905. Only a few traces of these structures remain.

The GPS position recorded was taken with its mountain backdrop matching the photos by North (1905) and McDonald (1951). Also, the several tombs, walls of quarried stone, and a number of adobe mounds indicate that the last mission site must have occupied this place.

Above left: *The ruins of the mission and several tombs were photographed in 1951 by Howard Gulick.*

Left: *A few hundred yards up this road through the village, the mission remnants are found on the left.*

Misión La Purísima Concepción de María de Cadegomó

It is likely that this acequia, which follows the road for several miles, was an original mission-era structure rebuilt to serve the modern day Ejido of San Ysidro.

An extensive irrigation system in the flat canyon bottom provided water for citrus, date, and olive trees, and many acres of grapes. These gardens produced a surplus of crops used to help sustain residents at less fortunate mission sites. Large quantities of wine and brandy were made at *La Purisíma,* and perhaps became a "cash crop" for the mission. Excellent dates are still grown in the canyon and sold throughout the south of the peninsula.

The population at its peak exceeded 2,000 after Indians were imported from Cedros Island, but suffered the usual decline caused by epidemics of measles and smallpox introduced by the Europeans. Syphilis, too, was transmitted to the Indians, and dramatically increased the infant mortality rate.

Even though the few remaining neophytes at *La Purísima* were supplemented by those moved from the mission at *Guadalupe* after its 1795 closure, only 54 Indians survived by 1800. The mission was abandoned in 1822; however, it must have continued to serve as a community church for many years, as Arthur North indicated that mass was still being held in the disintegrating church as late as 1905.

During our quest to find the remnants of this mission in 1997, we drove along the rolling coastal plain north of Villa Insurgentes. At the end of the paved road, we proceeded on an easily negotiated dirt road until it turned to the right up a flat canyon with a dry, sandy watercourse winding up the gentle slope of the arroyo. As we approached the village of La Purísima, the canyon walls increased in height and the foliage in the stream bottom became denser and beautifully green.

Misión La Purísima Concepción de María de Cadegomó

One of several tombs, and the wall in the photo at the above right, are located in the mission graveyard shown to the right in North's photo on page 74.

The cornerstones of this garden wall must have been gathered from the mission ruins.

We stopped at a schoolhouse on the outskirts of the village and approached to ask directions of the lady teacher (*maestra*). When I peered around the doorway opening, all sixteen children of this rural school stood and said in unison, "Hola señor, bienvenidos a nuestra clase": "Hello sir, welcome to our classroom." The maestra then greeted me and proceeded to ask me questions in Spanish much too rapidly for my limited skills.

I asked, "Muy despacio, por favor. Mi Español es muy malo." This plea, however, did not do much to slow down this very determined lady. We exchanged as much information as time would allow, and I was able to get enough details to enable our group to later find the the scattered remains of the mission.

Although there are few remnants of this once important mission, the beautiful valley, the friendly people, and the pleasure of visiting one more Baja California mission site made the trip most enjoyable.

Misión La Purísima Concepción de María de Cadegomó

Kino and Piccolo must have seen this view after crossing the Sierra Giganta. The live stream in the lush valley floor threads its way southwestward past Cerro Pilón toward the Pacific. The mission was a few miles downstream from this distinctive landmark.

1720 – 1748

Misión Nuestra Señora del Pilar
de la Paz Airapí

FOUNDED BY FATHERS JUAN DE UGARTE, S.J. & JAIME BRAVO, S.J.

N 24° 09.703'   W 110° 18.782

Misión Nuestra Señora del Pilar de la Paz Airapí

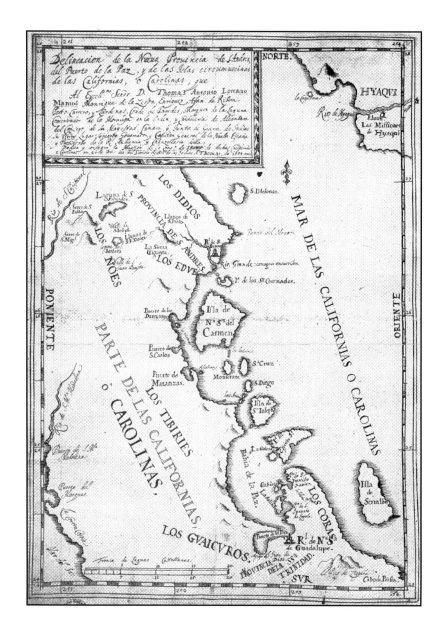

The beautiful and historic Bay of La Paz is shown on this map made by Father Kino, famed priest, explorer, and cartographer, in 1683. Explorers and pearlers sought refuge here. The island of Espíritu Santo, just north of the bay, served as the hiding place for Father Taraval during the 1734 Pericú rebellion. American forces occupied the city of La Paz during the Mexican-American war.

Misión Nuestra Señora del Pilar de la Paz Airapí

The beautiful, protected bay at La Paz attracted Spanish conquistadors, explorers, pearlers, and, of course, Indians, long before the first successful mission was established in 1720 by Jesuit Fathers Jaime Bravo and Juan de Ugarte.

The bay had long been a magnet to various Indian groups in the South Cape area because of its shelter, access to the offshore islands, and abundance of edible sea life. Fish, clams, and scallops were found, as well as oysters that not only provided tasty food but also yielded the prized pearl used by the natives as jewelry.

The first Spaniards to land near the bay were a Cortés-sponsored group of explorers who, after murdering their captain in a mutiny, were set upon by the Indians as they sought refuge and water in 1533. Those sailors who escaped to the mainland brought tales of the scores of pearls that could be obtained from the natives and the sea.

Cortés himself returned two years later with a force of 500, including soldiers; colonists, a few with families, lured by the tales of the wondrous pearls worn by the Indians; and the desire to establish a *pueblo* in this promising area. He too was thwarted by the scarcity of water and the hostility of the natives. The site was abandoned and the colonists returned to the mainland within two years.

Sebastián Vizcaíno, the famed captain of several seaborne explorations, tried to colonize La Paz in 1596 but was driven out when the stockade he built, near Cortés's earlier camp, was ignited by a cooking fire.

A party led by Admiral Atondo accompanied by Father Kino attempted colonization in 1683. Because of supply problems and attacks brought on by brutality to the natives, it was also forced to leave.

In spite of this history of failure and conflict, Bravo, with the aid of the multitalented Father Juan de Ugarte, was able to pacify the indigenous population and permanently establish *Misión Nuestra Señora de la Paz* on November 3, 1720.

To found the mission on the bay of La Paz, some 120 miles south of the mother mission at Loreto, Ugarte, then President of the Missions, employed the

SALDANA

Hernán Cortés, conqueror of the Aztec empire and its capital, now called Mexico City, unsuccessfully tried to establish a colony on the beautiful bay of La Paz in 1535.

ship he had built at *Mulegé, El Triunfo de la Cruz*. Provisions, soldiers, and animals as well as the adventurous padres were transported to *La Paz* in the small ship. The voyage following the coast south from Loreto was completed in five days.

A separate party that departed from *San Juan Bautista de Ligüí* led by Father Clemente Guillén brought additional provisions, soldiers, and some 50 neo-phytes from Guillén's mission. Although this group traveled about the same dis-tance as the seaborne expedition, 120 miles, the trip took them 23 days. They were forced to construct trails for the pack animals and to hack their way through dense, thorn-covered brush and cactus blanketing the rocky mountain-ous terrain.

On the arrival of the overland group at *La Paz*, gifts were exchanged with the natives and temporary shelters and a church were built of available sticks, brush, and palm thatch. The location of this first mission church is not known, but most historians believe it was located near the present plaza and church in the center of modern La Paz.

Father Ignacio Tirsch, of Misión Santiago, 50 miles to the south, made this painting of the Indians near his mission. He captioned it, "How two California Indians killed a deer with arrows, how they skinned it in the field…"

At the time of the *Pericú* revolt in 1734, the padre in charge of the mission was the Scotsman Father William Gordon. As he was visiting *Loreto* at the time the *Pericú* sacked and burned *La Paz*, Gordon was unharmed. The mission was reestablished in 1736 after a military campaign conducted by forces brought into the Cape from the mainland made it safe to resume operations. A description of the type or number of

Misión Nuestra Señora del Pilar de la Paz Airapí

buildings that composed the mission complex is not available.

Because of the continued hostility of the Indians and a series of epidemics, the mission was never again fully functional after the *Pericú* revolt. In 1748, the depleted Indian population and the name *Misión Nuestra Señora del Pilar* was transferred to *Misión Santa Rosa de las Palmas* near Todos Santos and the mission at La Paz abandoned.

Although unsuccessful as a mission location, La Paz has become the center for government and the most important commercial center in Baja California Sur. The bay, pleasant waterfront, and the interesting history make La Paz a very attractive city to visit.

At the plaza in the center of La Paz, this modern church may be located over the foundations of the ill-fated mission.

Misión Nuestra Señora del Pilar de la Paz Airapí

A point of land that protects one of the many deep coves that indent the shore of the island of Espíritu Santo is seen from shallow water. Padre Taraval of the mission at Todos Santos took refuge on the island during the Pericú revolt.

1720 – 1795

Misión Nuestra Señora de Guadalupe de Huasinapí

FOUNDED BY FATHER EVERARDO HELEN, S.J.

N 26° 55.086' W 112° 24.393'

Misión Nuestra Señora de Guadalupe de Huasinapí

VERNON, 2000

The mission ruins, behind the modern building in the left foreground, overlook the arroyo and seem pressed into the flank of the mountain rising behind.

Misión Nuestra Señora de Guadalupe de Huasinapí

The mission was founded in 1720, near a canyon logged the previous year by Fathers Ugarte and Sistiaga during their harvesting of shipbuilding timber. Everardo Helen, a Jesuit of German origin, was chosen to establish this mission in the Sierra Giganta among a large number of native *rancherías*.

Nuestra Señora de Guadalupe had a short and difficult life as a mission, in spite of being located in some of the most populous lands in the peninsula. Initial conversion efforts were quite successful as by 1721, with the aid of Father Jaime Bravo, 2,000 children and infants were baptized in the extensive area served by the mission.

By 1726, after recovering from an onslaught of disease and a plague of locust that brought famine and sickness, more than 1,700 Indians living in 32 rancherías in the domain of the mission had been converted to Christianity. The collapse of the church in a hurricane took over 100 lives in 1744, and by 1768, disease had again taken its toll and the population had declined to 530. As only

MATHES, 1960

The small modern concrete block chapel in the foreground of the photo above is discernable in the photo to the left, taken 40 years later. Several ranch buildings seen in Mathes' photo are no longer standing. The later photo shows much more undergrowth on the site. Perhaps in 1960 the brush had been removed for agricultural purposes.

74 Indians remained alive in 1795, the mission was abandoned and the indigenous population transferred to *Misión La Purísima*, 60 miles to the southeast near the Pacific.

Food was always a problem at *Guadalupe* because of the scarcity of level land for cultivation, and the mission was quite dependent on supplies brought in from Loreto. *Guadalupe's* lands apparently were better suited to the hunting/gathering method of food procurement of the natives than to the European village/farm structure of the missions.

A typical mission complex appears to have been built, including a church, some sort of housing, terraced *huertas,* and an irrigation system. Substantial herds of livestock must have been raised, as several large stone corrals are located on the grounds.

Perhaps because of the short life of the mission, few records of the building program are available. Time and the elements have erased most of the remnants of the buildings that stood on the terraced flats about the central ruin that must have been the mission chapel.

This probably was the west wall of the chapel. An earlier photo circa 1955 shows the same wall and a nearly complete gable end wall of adobe forming the north side of the structure. Note the entryway on the far end of the wall.

The chapel's outline measures 20 by 70 feet, and adjacent foundation traces of what might have been a porch are visible on two sides. Flat pieces of fired clay tile found in the adobe dust within the building's walls indicate that the chapel was in all probability paved. The one standing chapel half-wall utilizes roughly rectangular stones that were shaped or chosen for proper laying. As no mortar was used, the wall was skillfully chinked with smaller stones to produce a relatively flat, plumb, straight surface.

Misión Nuestra Señora de Guadalupe de Huasinapí

Above: Many rock corrals are found in the arroyo south of the main building ruins. All are laid without mortar. Similar walls serve to enclose and terrace the many ancient garden plots in the area.

Right: An overgrown and shrub-filled pila's sidewall is seen near the bottom of the arroyo.

The foundations were typical, made by filling deep wide trenches with local stone. Most walls of this mission structure must have been of adobe and have since melted onto the surrounding soil. Only a few stone walls and corrals remain.

Several dams, the padres' usual ambitious water systems fed by a small perennial stream, and the acres of mission garden lands created by stone-terraced walls attest to the labor-intensive efforts to produce sufficient food.

After Guadalupe's padres converted 32 rancherías, most Indians were transferred to the care of nearer missions at *Mulegé* and *San Ignacio*. *Guadalupe* retained responsibility for the balance, and built five *visitas* to serve these rancherías.

Small stone chapels were constructed at many outposts, and regular visits were made to baptize and bring the Indians into the faith. Now, only crumbling stone walls, graveyards, and building foundations remain at the sites. The nearest visita to *Guadalupe* is *San Miguel*, about 15 miles downstream on the Pacific watershed of Arroyo San Raymundo. Another, locally called *El Valle*, is located to the southwest in an *arroyo* that also flows to the Pacific. Ruins of a third, *San Patricio*, located partway to *Mulegé*, were obliterated by grading for roads.

The most noteworthy event in this remote canyon occurred in 1719, when Juan de Ugarte, the multitalented, hardworking priest from *San Javier*, logged a stand of *güéribo* trees in the arroyo to make lumber for a ship called *El Triunfo de la Cruz*. This was truly an amazing undertaking as, after the trees were felled and trimmed, it was necessary to drag the logs, using oxen and men, some 50 miles over the peninsular divide and down Arroyo Magdalena to the *estero* at Mulegé.

Under the supervision of a master shipwright, William Strafford, an English sea captain who spent many years on the Sea of Cortés, the logs were made into lumber, and the ship was built in a makeshift shipyard on the shore and launched in the quiet waters of the inlet. Considering that only the crudest tools were available, this shipbuilding feat must have required thousands of hours of backbreaking labor as well as great skill and knowledge.

These graves and the partial stone wall are all that remain of San Miguel, one of several visiting stations of Misión Guadalupe.

The ship, whose exact configuration is unknown, described as a 50-foot-long "bark-balandra" by one historian, sailed for years shuttling supplies along the gulf coast and bringing provisions from the mainland to the often hungry missionaries and Indians.

Arroyo Guadalupe is quite pretty, with many clumps of palms alongside the grass- and brush-choked streambed. The precipitous cactus- and lava-covered mountains on both sides of the arroyo make a striking contrast to the lush green canyon.

Misión Nuestra Señora de Guadalupe de Huasinapí

Above: *The old adobe ranch house, one-quarter mile from the mission, appears to have occasional use. It probably serves as shelter for the local cowboys when running livestock in the area.*

C.E. VERNON

Right: *Hot coals are piled into the depressions in a mortar-covered bench to give this backcountry stove "high, medium and low" capability.*

The watercourse of the mission arroyo falls toward the Pacific; however, only a few miles north after crossing the peninsular divide, Arroyo Magdalena is encountered. This scenic canyon, which falls to the gulf, is extensively farmed and winds past the standing ruins of the later-dated *visita* of *Magdalena*.

It is hard to imagine the bustle of activity that must have taken place—the building of stone foundations, the making of adobe, the construction of dams, irrigation projects, and the training and indoctrination of the Indians. Now the only sounds heard are from livestock grazing in the area, the passing of an occasional rattling ranch truck down the dusty road, or the movement of a *vaquero* through the brush of this scenic arroyo.

The few ranchers in the arroyos near the mission ruins live in a simple manner, far removed from the forces of modern life, in a spectacularly beautiful but hostile landscape that could not be subdued by the padres.

91

Misión Nuestra Señora de Guadalupe de Huasinapí

*Modern white concrete grave monuments are mixed among old stone-covered graves
in the camposanto at Visita San Miguel.*

1721 – 1741

Misión Nuestra Señora de los Dolores de Apaté

FOUNDED BY FATHER CLEMENTE GUILLÉN, S.J.

N 25° 03.343' W 110° 53.055'

Misión Nuestra Señora de los Dolores de Apaté

The stone ruins and extensive foundations stand on an alluvial flat 50 feet above the green arroyo, guarded by the steep sierra to the west.

Misión Nuestra Señora de los Dolores de Apaté

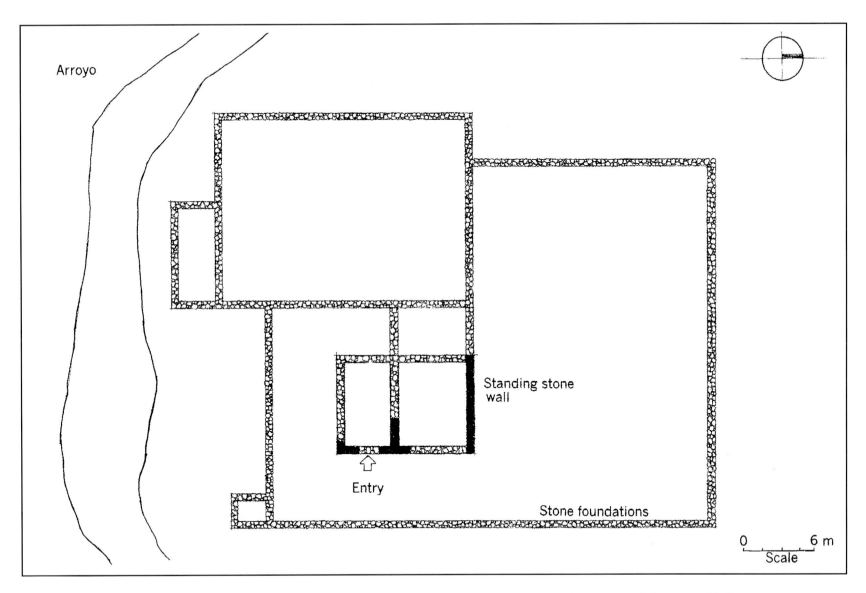

Arroyo

Standing stone wall

Entry

Stone foundations

0   6 m
Scale

Architect Salvador Hinojosa Oliva of La Paz developed this footprint of the ruins after a visit by helicopter in 1968.

Misión Nuestra Señora de los Dolores de Apaté

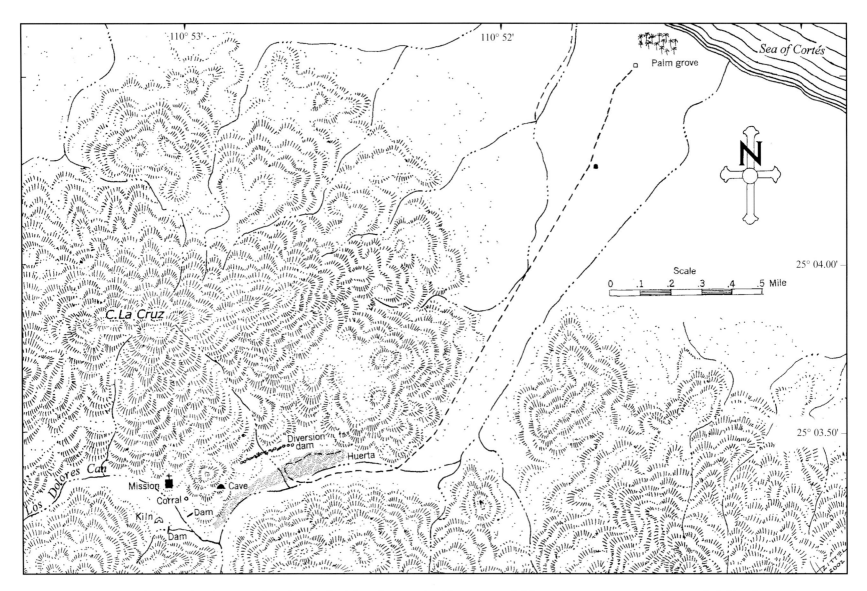

The mission, 2½ miles from the shore, is only a few hundred feet above sea level but surrounded by precipitous mountains that reach 1,500 feet in elevation.

Misión Nuestra Señora de los Dolores de Apaté

Father Clemente Guillén, while on an exploratory expedition in 1720, discovered a canyon on the Sea of Cortés called *Apaté* by the numerous *Guaycura* Indians living there. He returned to the site to found *Misión Nuestra Señora de los Dolores* in 1721, accompanied by the faithful Indians who had been forced to leave *Misión San Juan Bautista de Ligüí* by disease, lack of water, and attacks by rebellious natives.

The location, at the mouth of a broad sandy wash that faces the Sea of Cortés, is directly west of the northern tip of Isla San José. Water was available, either from the sometimes flowing spring-fed creek descending from the mountains to the west, or from shallow wells in the sandy creek bed. This water source helped sustain a large *ranchería* of Indians, and had provided water for over a century to the pearlers frequenting this coast as well as the earlier explorers prior to Father Guillén.

Records indicate that "a rude temple and a poor house" were constructed behind the beach at *Apaté,* perhaps near the building occupied by the present caretaker of Rancho Dolores, less than

Explorers and pearlers landed on this beach to find water by digging shallow pits that would soon fill with fresh water seeping down from the perennial springs in the canyon several miles from the shore. Here too, Father Guillén landed to found Misión Dolores in the year 1721.

one mile from the gulf. The well at the *rancho* taps the original water source for the mission; water is now found there at a depth of 60 feet.

Within 200 yards of the beach, behind a large clump of palms, stand the remains of a relatively spacious cement-floored, wood-frame and plastered house, probably built in about 1930 when considerable ranching and farming improvements were made in the *arroyo*. This building, scattered fruit trees, and additions to the mission's irrigation systems are remnants of several ranching endeavors carried on after the departure of the Indians and the missionaries.

The mission was moved inland in 1723 (the stone ruins 3 miles up the canyon must be remnants of the second site) because of salt water intrusion into the well near the gulf. There is no visible evidence of the original mission structures near the beach. The extensive permanent development farther up the arroyo indicates that this location was improved and occupied for many years.

In 1735, *Misión Dolores* served as headquarters for the assembly of a military force made up of *Yaqui* Indians from the mainland, recruited to help subdue the *Pericú* Indian uprising at the Cape that had resulted in the murder of two padres and had virtually destroyed the four southern missions. The use of *Dolores* as a staging area delayed a move to the better positioned *Visita la Pasión* from 1737 to 1741.

The crumbling ruins of *Misión Dolores* are on a flat by the side of a conical hill rising beside a winding, palm-lined arroyo. Although only a few walls are standing, several to a height

Above: *The lush green canyon behind the mission supplies a surprising amount of water to the highly developed system of acequias and pilas, which starts upstream to the west and continues down the widening canyon toward the gulf for several miles.*

Upper left: *Looking southwest, the front and side walls standing to full height can be seen. Note the twist in the sidewall that appears to be in danger of falling.*

Left: *The conical-shaped hill that marks the mission and storage cave stands to the northeast of the building ruins viewed from the edge of the arroyo behind the mission site.*

of 10 feet, foundations and stone rubble indicate that these mission buildings were composed of three or four rooms and covered an area of 100 by 150 feet.

The buildings were constructed of river stone and lava rock, all laid in mortar. The outline of several rooms are discernible by foundations and partial walls, and recesses high in the outer three walls appear to have been used to support roof rafters, indicating that a palm-thatched shed roof may have extended over the front and sides of the main building. No roofing tile remnants were found; however, flat stones were used to pave the porch areas.

One hundred and fifty feet east of the mission buildings, 3-foot-high dry-laid stone walls form a 60-foot-square enclosure that probably served as a corral.

Southwest of the ruins, across the bordering arroyo, is a lime kiln built into a 6-foot-high bench near the canyon wall. Cut stone has been laid as an outer shell and also lines a vertical semicircular excavation to form the well-like sides of the 3½-foot-diameter kiln.

A hundred yards from the kiln is a

stone dam/reservoir. The face crossing a steep arroyo must have been 60 feet long before one end was washed out by a torrential runoff. Mortared stones laid against a vertical cut on the slope of the mountain form one side of the 5-foot-high reservoir walls. The other wall was apparently carried off by the same flood that breached the dam. A wooden gate probably covered the rectangular slot in the face of the dam designed to discharge water through a stone trough to the canyon below. Perhaps a now washed-out *acequia* conducted water to the south side of the arroyo from the flared mouth of the discharge sluice protruding from the face of the dam.

Between the mission structures and the sandy arroyo bottom, another small stone dam was built to catch trickles of water from several springs. The pond behind the dam is about 30 feet in diameter and feeds a 30 by 45-foot *pila* less than one mile downstream and then, via another stone-lined acequia, waters the fields of a large *huerta* located on a bench above the creek bed.

The huerta is quite large and for over

Left: *The 16-foot-diameter semicircle cut in the face of the sandstone cliff marks the entry to a cool, dry 60-foot-deep cave that must have been excavated by Indian labor using crude iron hand tools. The interior was plastered to reduce seepage and the floor slopes slightly toward the door to allow drainage.*

Upper right: *The low "curbs" on each side of the central aisle are marked with shallow depressions that locals believe were used to position posts to support shelving for containers of wine and other provisions.*

Right: *The doorway in the flat-fired brick access wall utilizes a flat timber lintel probably not of mission fabrication. The brick could be of mission vintage, and the wall reconstructed during the ranching era.*

one mile follows the northwest bank of the arroyo bed toward the Sea of Cortés. A stone diversion dam, apparently to prevent storm runoff from eroding the huerta, was built below the mouth of the major side canyon crossing the huerta lands. Several large stone pilas and an extensive system of acequias indicate that great effort was expended to make this a productive agricultural center. The largest huerta is now a dry, dusty strip populated by scattered native shrubs. A few mango and citrus trees grow on the periphery, and brittle, gnarled grapevine trunks may be found in the sandy soil.

About one-quarter mile downstream from the mission, a large man-made cave was tunneled into the nearly vertical face of the mountain for a distance of 60 feet. This cave is said to have been used as a storeroom for the mission wine and other valuable crops. Flat-fired bricks wall off the front of the cave, and an iron barred grill seals the entry doorway.

Part of these lands, now Rancho Dolores, are cared for by Señor Lucio Amador, who lives there with his wife and four children in the 1930s house on the north side of the mouth of the canyon. They live off the land by raising goats, cattle, beans, and a few other seasonal crops.

The south side of the canyon and the grounds surrounding the mission ruins are claimed by Señor Arthur Moreno, who has fenced the mission grounds but left an opening to allow access by foot. Señor Moreno has cleaned a number of the acequias and added an extensive irrigation system of plastic pipe. It appears that the Moreno family intends to develop the property, as a stone-and-thatch *palapa* has been built near the mission dam, and a number of fruit trees, irrigated by a drip system, have been planted in the sandy arroyo bottom.

The site is quite isolated. The only visitors via land are an occasional *vaquero* who must ride or walk in from the highlands down a difficult trail, or the nearest gulfside neighbor at Rancho Los Burros may visit after a 10-mile hike. Fishermen frequent the area in their *pangas* to take on water, and recently kayak exploration trips have made Rancho Dolores one of their stops.

In 1741, the headquarters of *Misión Dolores* was moved in an effort to find more reliable water and to allow less rigorous passage to Loreto and San Luis Gonzaga. The site selected was 15 miles southwest, by a mountain arroyo on the Pacific slope with the Indian place name of *Chillá,* where a *visita* of *Misión Dolores,* called *La Pasión* by the Spanish, was sited. At the new location, *Misión los Dolores* was commonly called *"La Pasión."* The historical literature refers to a location called *Tañuetía* (*Place of the ducks*) as the second mission site. The author believes that the places called *Tañuetía, Chillá* and

Above: *A pila, which seems to always have water, is supplied by an acequia from the arroyo to the west and irrigates several gardens down the canyon. It is located a few hundred yards east and 50 feet lower than the mission.*

Left: *Miles of stone-and-mortar–lined acequias wind down the canyon. This canal near the mission has recently been cleaned, and delivers water to young fruit trees below.*

Misión Nuestra Señora de los Dolores de Apaté

Above: *The left half of the dam face has been carried away by a flood from the sharply rising canyon. Note the slot that must have been covered with a gate to control the downstream flow.*

Right: *Rocks may have been piled in this discharge flume to slow the flow of water to the irrigation system below.*

La Pasión are all very close to each other and define the area of the final site of *Misión Dolores*.

A typical dirt road from the southwest that passes the ruins of *La Pasión* leads to the rim of the deep canyon only 3 or 4 miles from the mission. A difficult climb for man or mule down into this canyon must be undertaken to reach *Misión Dolores* by this route.

Access from the sea is quite simple, provided the weather is benign. The fishing village of San Evaristo, 85 miles north of La Paz, is reached by 40 miles of paved highway from La Paz to the mining town of San Juan de la Costa, and an additional 45 miles of quite scenic, twisting dirt road to San Evaristo. This beautifully protected bay is the home of a fishing village, and *pangas* can be obtained for the hour-and-a-half ride to the beach below *Misión Dolores*.

The rugged isolated beauty of the canyon, the mission walls, gardens, cave, and elaborate water system afford a fascinating view of this lonely and historic site. It is well worth the journey to visit the place the natives called *Apaté*.

Misión Nuestra Señora de los Dolores de Apaté

Stones piled against the bank form the front side of the lime kiln. The back of the well-like construction was built into the hillside, and square-cut stones lined the cylindrical inner surface.

Mortar was used to strengthen the casing, as shown in the center photograph. To the right, Clark Vernon, one of our June 2001 party, stands on the crest of the hill and peers into the top of the horno.

Misión Nuestra Señora de los Dolores de Apaté

The mission is surrounded by steep rock walls cut by a few boulder-strewn watercourses plunging down from the mountains above.

Misión Nuestra Señora de los Dolores de Apaté

T. VERNON, 2001

The east-facing stone facade and arched entry are silhouetted against the late afternoon sky.

1724 – 1795

Misión Santiago el Apóstol Aiñiní

FOUNDED BY FATHER IGNACIO MARÍA NÁPOLI, S.J.

N 23° 28.516'   W 109° 43.066'

Father Tirsch painted this somewhat imaginative scene and titled it, "Santiago or the mission named after Saint Joseph in California which I almost completed."

Misión Santiago el Apóstol Aiñiní

Above: *The caption "The interior view of my church, which was named after Saint Jacob. However I had not quite completed it." may have overstated the grandeur and form of what was reported to be a flat brush-roofed adobe church.*

Left: *Tirsch, who was stationed at Santiago in 1767 when Portolá arrived to expel the Jesuits, sketched several churches, local inhabitants both native and Spanish, and also made drawings of plant and animal life. Although the architectural accuracy of drawings might be challenged, the drawings do reveal many interesting details of life at the missions during the Jesuit era.*

In a quest to expand the area served and to find new souls to save, the Jesuits determined that missions should be established south of La Paz in the Cape area, home of numerous Indians of several language groups.

The first choice was a beautiful location 60 miles southeast of La Paz on the shores of Bahía Las Palmas. Father Ignacio Nápoli journeyed there in 1721 to work among the *Coras,* but returned within a year without formally founding the mission because of supply and communication problems.

Nápoli next chose Santa Ana, the center for the most important mines on the peninsula, at a point in the mountains midway between La Paz and the beaches of the Cape. This site too was abandoned, as a sudden storm caused the collapse of a temporary stick-and-pole church that resulted in many injuries and loss of Indian life.

It was not until 1724 that Father Nápoli was able to return to the Cape area, at which time he selected a place 25 miles north of San José beside a broad *arroyo,* called *Aiñiní* by the natives, to found *Misión Santiago el Apóstol Aiñiní.*

There have been several sites in or near the charming village of Santiago. Rancho la Misión, several miles north of town, owned by the Cota family, is said to be built on the ruins of the mission. The two photographs on the next page picture a site on the plaza of Loma Sur in the village that is thought to be the final location of the mission.

The many problems that beset the southern missions persisted at *Aiñiní.* The most significant was the stubborn and fierce resistance of the *Pericú* and other southern indigenous groups to mission life, and their reluctance to accept the moral codes of Catholicism.

With the arrival of the padres and Spanish soldiers in the Cape area, the Indians were soon decimated by a series of epidemics, including measles and smallpox. As they were not resistant to these diseases, the indigenous population rapidly declined. Many of the women died or were made sterile by syphilis, forcing the birth rate to decline dramatically, further impacting the diminishing population. The banning of polygamy by the priests exacerbated friction as the Indians were loath to give up this long-standing and perhaps necessary practice of their hunting and gathering society.

Restrictions placed on the Indians' age-old habit of roaming and moving their *ranchería* area often, and many other cultural conflicts, led to frequent instances of disobedience to the padres' orders, and in 1734, widespread Indian discontent led to a general revolution in the South Cape area.

Above right: *Englehardt captioned this J. R. Slevin photo, "Church of Mission Santiago in 1919." The location of this ruin is not indicated, but it must have been the last mission building, and may have been at the same location as the later brick church below.*

Right: *During his 1950 jeep trip, McDonald wrote, "…we found the third mission in the south part of town, known as Loma Sur. A small brick church was being constructed over the remains, and there was little evidence that a mission had occupied the site, except for the bells which were mounted on some poles in front of the new church."*

Misión Santiago el Apóstol Aiñiní

Santiago was the first of the four southern missions attacked by the rebels. Father Carranco was seized and murdered on October 1, 1734. The mission was sacked and burned and Father Carranco's body was thrown on the flaming heap of mission possessions.

The marauders proceeded to *San José* a few days later, and both the priest and mission suffered the same fate. The rebels also destroyed *Misión Santa Rosa de las Palmas* near Todos Santos, but fortunately the priest there, Father Taraval, who had been warned by loyal Indians, escaped the raiding party.

In 1736, a rebuilding program was started at *Santiago*. However, the padres and the few soldiers assigned to protect the mission were continuously harassed by minor uprisings, runaways, and continued epidemics.

The Indian population, which was estimated at 350 in 1745, varied quite radically throughout the Jesuit era, depending on the ability of the mission to replenish Indians lost in epidemics with natives from other peninsular areas.

The Dominicans, who took over the administration of *Santiago* after the expulsion of the Jesuits, did not fare much better, and by 1795 it was necessary to abandon the mission; the few surviving Indians were sent to *Misión San José*.

The village of Santiago has survived and now flourishes as a most pleasant locale surrounded by small farms growing avocados and mangoes, as well as a large variety of other fruit and vegetables. This commercial center for the ranches in the area still occupies the final site of the mission, two hills named Loma Norte and Loma Sur.

The modern church built in 1958 on Loma Sur now serves the community at Santiago, and is built over the ruins of the brick church shown on page 110, which was destroyed by a hurricane. According to local lore, this is also the final site of the mission church. Rock walls in an arroyo next to the church are said to be remnants of the mission Indian dwellings.

San Ignacio Sector Map

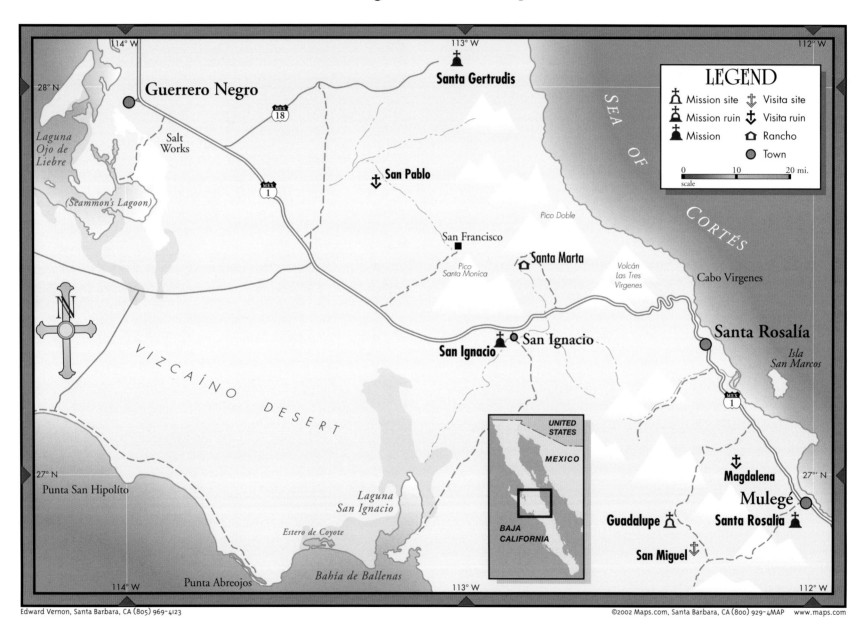

Santa Gertrudis

Guerrero Negro

SEA OF CORTÉS

Laguna Ojo de Liebre

Salt Works

LEGEND

Mission site   Visita site
Mission ruin   Visita ruin
Mission   Rancho
       Town

0   10   20 mi.
scale

(Scammon's Lagoon)

San Pablo

Pico Doble

San Francisco

Santa Marta

Volcán
Las Tres
Vírgenes

Pico
Santa Mónica

Cabo Virgenes

Santa Rosalía

Isla
San Marcos

San Ignacio

San Ignacio

VIZCAÍNO DESERT

UNITED STATES

MEXICO

Punta San Hipólito

Magdalena

Mulegé

Laguna
San Ignacio

BAJA
CALIFORNIA

Guadalupe

Santa Rosalía

Estero de Coyote

San Miguel

Punta Abreojos

Bahía de Ballenas

Edward Vernon, Santa Barbara, CA (805) 969-4123   ©2002 Maps.com, Santa Barbara, CA (800) 929-4MAP   www.maps.com

1728 – 1840

Misión Nuestro Señor San Ignacio
de Kadakaamán

FOUNDED BY FATHER JUAN BAUTISTA DE LUYANDO, S.J.

N 27° 17.023' W 112° 53.905'

Misión Nuestro Señor San Ignacio de Kadakaamán

VERNON

A view of the mission across the former vineyard.

Misión Nuestro Señor San Ignacio de Kadakaamán

A beautiful valley at the base of forbidding lava-covered mountains with its many native *Cochimí* Indians was first discovered by Father Francisco Piccolo, a Jesuit priest based at *Misión Santa Rosalía de Mulegé*. He visited the palm-lined lakeside site, known to the Indians as *Kadakaamán*, in November 1706, during an expedition to find populous Indian *rancherías* and promising locations for missions.

It was desired to promptly establish a mission at this site because of plentiful water, ample area for agriculture, and numerous natives. However, only periodic visits to teach the Catholic faith were possible because of the shortage of priests.

In January 1728, Father Juan Bautista de Luyando, a priest newly arrived in Baja California, set out from Loreto for the *arroyo* with a party of nine mounted soldiers, many Indian neophytes, and a supply laden train of pack animals. He arrived at the site later the same month to formally establish *Misión Nuestra Señor San Ignacio de Kadakaamán*.

The ornate and beautiful Moorish motif church faces the plaza of the peaceful, charming village of San Ignacio.

PLOCH

115

Misión Nuestro Señor San Ignacio de Kadakaamán

Viewed from the south, the church, courtyard wall, and outbuildings have a fortress-like appearance.

The stairway leading to the choir loft up the north side of the church appears to have been widened. It must have been precariously narrow when first made.

The substantial stone church was preceded by stick huts and later by adobe buildings. The exact date when the stone buildings were commenced is not clear. However, in 1786 under Dominican administration, Father Juan Gómez completed the building of the beautiful structures that survive today.

In its early history, *San Ignacio* was directed for many years by the Jesuit Sebastián de Sistiaga, aided by the adventurous explorer Father Fernando Consag, who is sometimes credited with commencing the stone church. It was from here, in 1747, that Consag launched the exploration that discovered several *rancherías* and a spring called *Cadacamán,* 60 miles to the north, where *Misión Santa Gertrudis* was eventually located.

Initially there were probably several thousand natives in the area administered by *San Ignacio,* and its converts came from distances as far as Cedros Island. Jesuit records, commenced in 1728, indicate that by 1758, more than 2,000 baptisms were recorded. However, the population decreased from 558 in 1771, to 305 in 1774. By 1800, only 130 "souls" survived the diseases brought to the peninsula by the Europeans.

In spite of the incessant loss of life, *San Ignacio* was extremely productive agriculturally. Hundreds of gallons of wine were produced each year, as well as figs, olives, pomegranates, sugarcane, and other valuable garden crops.

These round windows, on the left and right of the facade, are individually decorated with dark-colored carved stonework.

The detailed paneled door of the main entry is nearly 20 feet high and surrounded by intricate carved stonework.

Christ, as depicted by this statue, is the centerpiece of the altar to the left of the nave, and one of the most impressive pieces of statuary found in this highly decorated church.

The retablo, or altarpiece, must have been constructed in Mexico of many carved wooden pieces, covered with gold leaf, then transported to the mission and assembled on site. The paintings surrounding the centerpiece were probably done in the 18th century.

This beautiful statue of the Virgin of Guadalupe adorns the altar to the right of the central nave.

Saint Ignatius, the centerpiece of the retablo, looks down the central aisle of the church toward the main entry and the village plaza.

Misión Nuestro Señor San Ignacio de Kadakaamán

Right: *Cone-like "pináculos" stand on the cornice over statues of saints and angels who view the plaza from niches in the facade of the beautiful old church.*

Far right: *A stairway to a wall pulpit is housed by the castle-like quarter-round tower.*

Below center: *Niches with statues of saints are below the angels and on either side of the main entry.*

Below: *This doorway opens to the cross aisle of the nave. A matching doorway provides access from the other side.*

Misión Nuestro Señor San Ignacio de Kadakaamán

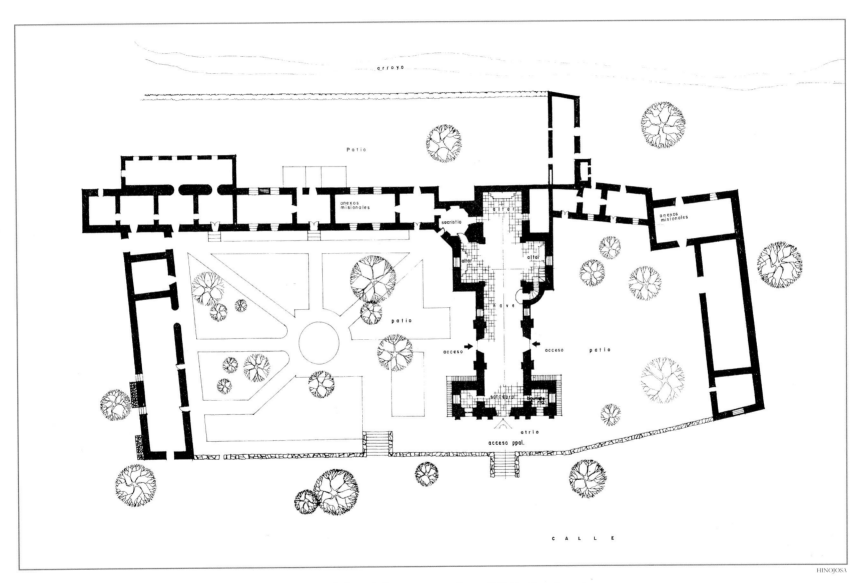

Plan view of the existing stone complex at Misión San Ignacio.

HINOJOSA

121

Misión Nuestro Señor San Ignacio de Kadakaamán

One of the most interesting projects at *San Ignacio* during the mission era was "The Grand Muralla," a dike nearly 3 miles long. Built of boulders, rocks, sand, and earth, this structure was made to protect the mission and its growing grounds from the infrequent but powerful floods that raged down the canyons to devastate the crops in the fields surrounding the mission. It can still be clearly seen, as the road that approaches the village from the highway cuts through the dike just below the reed-lined lake. From that point it curves to the east and becomes tangent to the road leading to Santa Rosalía, about 2 miles from the mission.

The dike was reported to originally have been nearly 12 feet high, 40 feet wide at its base, and 3 miles long. This truly is an amazing structure, particularly when it is considered that all the labor was done by hand by Indians using no more than the crude tools of the day, and with the aid of oxen and mules.

Lava boulders piled to a height of about 8 feet form this portion of the dike. Note that a few small homes have been built on the "dry" side of the barrier.

Misión Nuestro Señor San Ignacio de Kadakaamán

In spite of over 250 years of erosion and weather, portions of the structure may easily be followed along the river bottom, past several homes, angling toward the highway to eventually fade into an *arroyo* several miles from the village.

The mission was abandoned in 1840 because all of the Indian population had died. Now, however, it is the vital center of the small village of San Ignacio under the able guidance of Padre James Donald Francez of the Camboyan order.

Certainly *San Ignacio* is one of the most interesting and well-preserved monuments of the mission era in Baja California. It is a standing tribute to the great builders, both religious and native, who worked so long and diligently to create this wonderful structure.

Located mid-peninsula between Guerrero Negro and Santa Rosalía, the mission is only a mile or so off the main highway. The quaint colonial village, the palm groves, and the beautiful lake would make this stop worthwhile even without the added bonus of the lovely old mission.

At this location, the embankment is built primarily of river rock, sand, and gravel. Here it crosses a side canyon, and in many places is nearly concealed by shrubs and undergrowth.

Misión Nuestro Señor San Ignacio de Kadakaamán

It is a delightful surprise to suddenly have this lake pop into view after crossing the hot arid Vizcaíno desert. Water from the high lava-strewn mountains to the north eventually filters down to form the palm-fringed lake, which is the "reason for being" for Misión San Ignacio, one-half mile downstream.

1730 – 1840

Misión San José del Cabo Añuití

FOUNDED BY FATHER NICOLÁS TAMARAL, S.J.

N 23° 02.947'   W 109° 41.538'

ALEXANDER–JEAN NOËL

Life and death at the mission during the 1769 typhus epidemic was drawn with almost photographic accuracy by the French artist Noël.

Misión San José del Cabo Añuití

TIRSCH/J. CROSBY

Above: *Padre Ignacio Tirsch, the Jesuit priest at Santiago, painted this romanticized view of the mission at San José and captioned his work, "San José del Cabo, another mission named after Saint Joseph in the foothills of San Lucas, in California, which was also nearly completed by me." The mission is depicted circa 1765, with the Philippine ship arriving to be supplied with food.*

Left: *Noël, a member of the Spanish-French expedition led by Abbé Chappe d'Auteroche to observe the transit of Venus, made this realistic drawing showing the gritty life at the mission. Note that most of the buildings appear to be of reeds with palm-thatch roofs except the main building that may have had walls of adobe. The site probably is on or near the present location of the church in the pueblo of San José. Courtesy of Réunion des Musées Nationaux/Art Resource, New York.*

Father Nicolás Tamaral, in 1730, first established *Misión San José del Cabo Añuití* near the beach and the beautiful verdant *estero* formed by an underground stream flowing from the craggy mountain range 10 miles inland from the East Cape shore. Initially the mission must have been quite successful, as Father Tamaral proudly mentioned in his correspondence that 1,034 Indians were baptized in the first year.

Although the exact location of the stick, brush and palm-frond *jacals* that served as the first church and padre's *casa* is not known, the site was soon moved 5 miles inland to a plain on the edge of an *arroyo* in the present location of the village of San José Viejo.

Remnants of the adobe church at San José Viejo were visible in 1978 when Robertson reported that "…the few foundation walls of the mission are incorporated into the ranch home." McDonald's 1951 photo of what is presumed to be the same ranch house states that, according to its residents, it is built on mission foundations.

Misión San José del Cabo Añuití

Left: *A 17th-century galleon as it may have appeared when preparing to anchor off the shore of the estero behind San Bernabé Bay to take on water. The first galleon to be provisioned by the mission at San José arrived early in 1734.*

Below: *The estero, which now abuts a modern resort hotel, first attracted Indians, then explorers, pirates, the famous Manila galleon, and missionaries to partake of its fresh water. Located 25 miles northeast of Los Arcos at the tip of the Cape near the pueblo of San José, the plain above the estero once was a site of Misión San José del Cabo.*

Misión San José del Cabo Añuití

The annual galleon, sailing between Manila and the port of Acapulco on the west coast of the mainland of New Spain, paid its first visit to the mission located near the shore of San Bernabé Bay in January 1734. The nearby estero offered precious water and the mission provided much-needed fresh meat, fruit, and vegetables to the scurvy-stricken and nearly starved crew.

Misión San José was destroyed, as were all four of the southern missions, during the October 1734 *Pericú* revolt. Father Tamaral, unable to escape, was murdered then burned by the insurgents. The mission's location was moved back toward the gulf in 1735. Local lore and an INAH monument places it by the old cemetery on a low bluff within a few hundred yards of the beach, one-quarter mile from the edge of the estero.

By 1736, the revolutionaries were sufficiently subdued by Spanish military forces from the mainland to allow the ravaged mission to resume operations at its new site as a *visita* under the administration of the mission at Santiago. A *presidio* with 10 soldiers, to protect Spanish interests in the area, was also established at San José.

According to McDonald, this ranch house on the edge of a small canyon in the village of San José Viejo is built on the foundations of the first site of the mission. Gerhard & Gulick and Robertson confirmed a similar site during their visits nearly 50 years ago. The author was unable to find this building in a 1999 search.

Misión San José del Cabo Añuití

The church on the plaza at San José was severely damaged in the cyclone of 1918. The present twin-towered church was built on the same location in 1932. This site may also have been the place where the last mission church was located.

Mathes indicates that in 1753 the mission was moved one mile inland from the beachside (cemetery site) to its third location at what was to become the pueblo of San José. On November 30, 1767, after a storm-tossed 40-day voyage from the mainland, Captain Gaspar de Portolá landed below the mission on the broad curve of the sandy beach of San Bernabé Bay. His purpose was to proceed to *Loreto* and carry out the king's orders to expel all Jesuit priests from Baja California.

As there was no priest at the few buildings standing at San José, Portolá made contact with Father Ignacio Tirsch at *Misión Santiago*, 20 miles to the north. He demanded aid in procuring the supplies needed by his party to make their way overland to the missions' headquarters at Loreto, more than 300 miles to the northwest.

Until the Dominican era, *San José* functioned primarily as a military station and farm to supply the Manila galleon as well as other peninsula missions. A small community of soldiers, their families, and sufficient neophytes (50 were counted in 1769) to provide the labor necessary to raise crops and herd cattle, resided on the mission grounds.

According to Englehardt, the population continued to decline and in 1782, during the early Dominican era, only 25 neophytes were under the charge of the church. The population increased considerably when, on the closing of *Misión Santiago* in 1795, its remaining Indians were transferred to *San José*.

The mission was destroyed by a flood in 1793 and not rebuilt until 1799.

Misión San José del Cabo Añuití

, were
second,
uarters
n. The
laza of
opula-
sion in
ve been
its have

broke
era, and
an naval
ned mis-
osition.
ed the
like mis-
brought
he siege,
intained
ter peace
1848.
rt of La
mission-
by Vicar
ls to visit
ns, which
es.

This twin-towered church serves the community of San José del Cabo. A tile representation of the killing of Father Tamaral is located over the main entry door.

The church at San José was described as "but a jacal (stick) structure." Even so, 220 persons were confirmed during Escalante's visit, none of them reported to be Indians. The mission era had truly ended in the South Cape.

After the mission days and the Mexican-American war, the area grew in importance as an agricultural and ranching center. San José today is thriving and part of the tourist development on the South Cape. It is hoped that this new boom does not completely erase the character and tranquil feel of the picturesque and historic colonial village.

Misión San José del Cabo Añuití

The scene depicted on painted tiles over the main entry of the church at San José del Cabo shows Father Tamaral being dragged to a fire by rebel Pericú Indians. This incident took place on October 3, 1734, during the general uprising of the South Cape natives.

1733 – 1840

Misión Santa Rosa de las Palmas*

FOUNDED BY FATHER SIGISMUNDO TARAVAL, S.J.

N 23° 27.621'   W 110° 13.115'

* CALLED MISIÓN NUESTRA SEÑORA DEL PILAR AFTER 1748
RESETTLEMENT OF INDIANS FROM LA PAZ. ABANDONED THEN
REESTABLISHED CIRCA 1825 IN VILLAGE PLAZA 1 MILE SOUTH.

Misión Santa Rosa de las Palmas

This modern church was built in 1970 by the Camboyan fathers on the site of the original Jesuit mission.

Misión Santa Rosa de las Palmas

In 1724, on the banks of a shallow *arroyo* 4 miles from the Pacific shore, a visiting station was established by Jesuit Father Jaime Bravo near the outskirts of the present town of Todos Santos. This site functioned as a mission farm and center for the conversion of the *Pericú* Indians native to the area under the supervision of *Misión Nuestra Señora del Pilar*, located in La Paz 50 miles to the north.

Ample surface water was usually available from a reed-lined, spring-fed creek. Many acres of flat land suitable for farming followed the waterway to the Pacific—an unusual and fortunate find on the most often dry and barren Pacific shore of the peninsula.

A grant from the wealthy and devout family of the Marqués de Villapuente in 1733 enabled the *visita* to be elevated to mission status. Father Sigismundo Taraval, a young priest of aristocratic Spanish heritage, was put in charge. The mission was named *Santa Rosa de las Palmas* after Doña Rosa de la Peña, the sister-in-law of the Marqués.

At the time of Taraval's arrival, many of the *Pericú* Indians had recently died from a severe smallpox epidemic. Shortly thereafter, in 1734, the *Pericú,* angry because of the drastic lifestyle restrictions—particularly the ban against polygamy—imposed by the padres, revolted, which resulted in

Above right: *The porch and patio of the house built on the old mission grounds is supported on a dry-laid stone wall that was probably built by mission Indian labor.*

Right: *Mission walls or foundation stones are used to help form a lube pit and car wash.*

Misión Santa Rosa de las Palmas

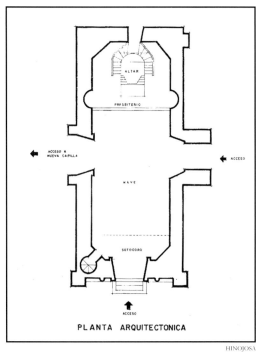

Howard Gulick, well-known Baja California explorer and author, took this photo of the old Dominican adobe plaza church in 1949. Its plan is shown by the drawing to the right.

the destruction and abandonment of the four southern missions at *La Paz, Todos Santos, San José,* and *Santiago.*

The priests at the missions *San José* and *Santiago* were murdered, each at their own mission (stabbed repeatedly, shot with arrows, beaten, then burned), by the rampaging Indians. Father Taraval reluctantly left his mission at the urging of several mission guards who had heard of the revolt from faithful converts. The escape party fled across the peninsula at night to La

Paz to avoid the rebels. There they found the mission in ruins, and in order to prevent capture by the angry natives, fled by canoe to the island of Espíritu Santo, a few miles offshore in the Sea of Cortés.

One year later, Father Taraval returned to *Santa Rosa* to reinstate the process of religious conversion and acculturation of the gentiles. A military troop of Spanish soldiers and loyal Indians was brought into the lower peninsula from New Spain,

Misión Santa Rosa de las Palmas

and fought for several years to protect the missions and subdue the revolution. However, *Santa Rosa* continued to suffer additional attacks from the warlike *Pericú*, and also was inflicted with a series of plagues. Even after the 1748 closing of *Misión Nuestra Señora del Pilar de la Paz* and the relocation of its *Guaycura* Indians to *Santa Rosa,* the mission made little progress. The population in 1762 was only 90, more than 29 years after it had been formally founded.

In 1768, after replacement of the Jesuits by Franciscans, Visitador-General Gálvez closed the missions of *San Luis Gonzaga* and *Dolores* and forced the transfer of their 800 *Guaycura* Indians to the mission beside the fertile, verdant arroyo of Todos Santos. This move further exacerbated the resentment of the natives, and as a result, many Indians fled to return to their distant home territory or the mountains to live in their traditional manner.

Frequent sorties of soldiers and loyal neophytes were required to capture the escapees and return them, by force if necessary, to the mission compound. In order to deter the Indians' inclination to desert, the friars took the severe measure of detaining their children. To add to the calamities that befell the native population, an epidemic of measles killed 300 neophytes less than one year after they had been transplanted by Gálvez. By the year 1800, desertion and disease had reduced the Indian population to fewer than 200.

The name *Nuestra Señora del Pilar* was applied to *Misión Santa Rosa* after the 1748 closing of *Misión Nuestra Señora del Pilar de La Paz*. It is likely that *Santa Rosa* was never fully re-

The window opening into the choir loft is directly over what was the main entry into the mission church. This small chapel, 16 by 58 feet, is now the entry into the nave of the parish church, Nuestra Señora del Pilar de Todos Santos.

built after the *Pericú* revolt. A number of different priests served for short intermittent periods, and the buildings as well as the congregation must have continued to deteriorate.

In 1825, a young Dominican friar, Father Gabriel González, was assigned to Todos Santos, and it is possible that he took the responsibility to build the new church on what is now the plaza of the *pueblo* one mile south of the first site. Although

Misión Santa Rosa de las Palmas

This beautiful niche and statue of Christ is in the wall to the left of the altar.

An old altar on the west end of the 1825 mission chapel faces the original choir loft and main entry.

The nave and the main aisle of the "new" church from the cross aisle of the chapel.

few records are available, the current priest Víctor Refugio López does have baptismal records dating back to 1837. It is likely that the foyer of the plaza church was built before that time and was the final mission church.

As the number of neophytes continued to shrink, there was no choice but to close the mission in 1840. However, the church continued to function as a parish church, and González eventually became president in charge of all the Dominican churches on the peninsula.

The original portion of the plaza church was built of adobe in a simple rectangular style with the choir loft over the entry, an altar at the opposite end, and a flat-beamed ceiling, very much like earlier mission churches. In 1967, a new concrete building to create a larger nave was added perpendicular to the side of the old Dominican structure. The side door under the bell tower of the old chapel then became the entry for the new church. The original choir loft and altar can be seen at opposite ends of what is now the foyer.

The location of the first mission buildings, one mile north of town, can be identified by a modern church built among the ruins of *Misión Santa Rosa de las Palmas*. Behind the church, a local family that has lived on the site for several generations operates a car wash bordered by mission walls and foundation remnants. Their home, on a gentle rise behind the modern church, is placed so that the front porch is supported by what must have been a stone mission wall. The use of rocks and stone from the fallen mission makes it certain that all evidence of it will soon be obliterated.

Early in the 20th century, the pueblo of Todos Santos experienced a boom economy brought on by a new sugar mill built to process the sugarcane that has been grown in the area since the days of the mission. New commercial development in the village includes a movie theater, hotel, and ballpark. The sugar mill is now deserted and in ruins, but a tall smokestack still stands as well as a number of foundations and deteriorating brick walls as

The bell tower facing the plaza now serves as the main entry to the church. It was constructed as the principal adornment and side entry to the mission chapel built by the Dominicans circa 1825.

monuments to the brief days of industrial and commercial development.

The surrounding farms produce a variety of fruit and vegetables in fields rimmed with palms. The 19th-century buildings now used as shops and restaurants give this small pueblo a romantic and peaceful ambience. Perhaps the spirits of the padres and Indians add to the tranquillity of this charming locale.

Misión San Luis Gonzaga Sector Map

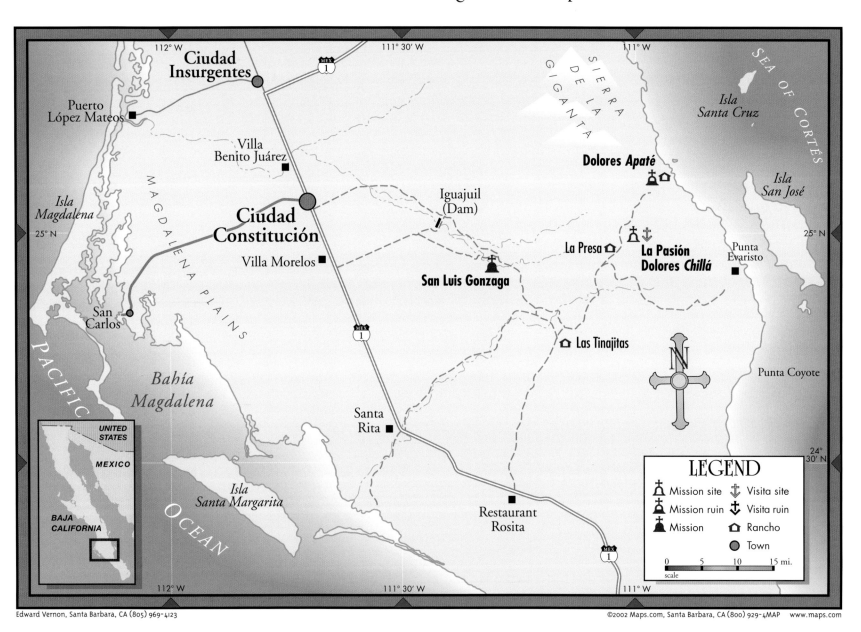

112° W

111° 30' W

111° W

Ciudad Insurgentes

Puerto López Mateos

Villa Benito Juárez

Isla Magdalena

25° N

Ciudad Constitución

Villa Morelos

San Carlos

MAGDALENA PLAINS

Bahía Magdalena

PACIFIC

Isla Santa Margarita

OCEAN

S I E R R A D E L A G I G A N T A

Isla Santa Cruz

SEA OF CORTÉS

Dolores *Apaté*

Iguajuil (Dam)

Isla San José

La Presa

La Pasión Dolores *Chillá*

Punta Evaristo

25° N

San Luis Gonzaga

Las Tinajitas

Santa Rita

Punta Coyote

N

Restaurant Rosita

24° 30' N

LEGEND

Mission site   Visita site

Mission ruin   Visita ruin

Mission   Rancho

Town

0   5   10   15 mi.
scale

UNITED STATES

MEXICO

BAJA CALIFORNIA

112° W

111° 30' W

111° W

Edward Vernon, Santa Barbara, CA (805) 969-4123

1737 – 1768

Misión San Luis Gonzaga Chiriyaqui

FOUNDED BY FATHER LAMBERTO HOSTELL, S.J.

N 24° 54.518' W 111° 17.429'

Misión San Luis Gonzaga Chiriyaqui

PLOCH, 1998

This simple, well-preserved stone church stands on the Magdalena Plain, 30 miles south of Ciudad Constitución.

Misión San Luis Gonzaga Chiriyaqui

isión San Luis Gonzaga is often overlooked because of its simplicity or perhaps because of its short life. Though it appears to be plain and modest, particularly when compared to the "jewels" of the Jesuits' creations, such as *San Javier* and *San Ignacio*, this mission stands with lonely dignity on a plain above a usually live stream in a wide desolate valley.

It was first established as a *visita* for *Misión Dolores Apaté*, then administered by Father Clemente Guillén; an endowment by the Count of Santiago, Don Luis Velasco, enabled its establishment as a mission in 1737, under the charge of the 31-year-old German priest, Father Lamberto Hostell.

In 1751, a new appointee, Austrian Jesuit Jacob Baegert, made a six-month journey from Mexico City to his assignment at *San Luis Gonzaga*. As other transportation was not available, the difficult gulf crossing was made in a canoe with a *Yaqui* Indian crew. On arrival Baegert found that a hurricane had destroyed nearly all the mission structures, and he had to commence rebuilding them. The twin-towered stone church that still stands today was started at that time.

The church was built of local sandstone with a rosy hue, set in mortar to form sturdy walls. The front of the church, as well as the towers, the

Above: *The church and surrounding buildings form a plaza in front of the low stone dam.*

Left: *The deserted building across the plaza from the mission was probably built in the late 1800s, and served as a mansion or ranch headquarters on an independently owned cattle ranch after secularization.*

VERNON, 1998

A side view shows the sturdy and enduring qualities of the stonework construction.

Misión San Luis Gonzaga Chiriyaqui

interior, and the ceiling, were plastered to a smooth finish. Fired adobe bricks (Baegert had 30,000 made on site) were used to form the ceiling vault, which is supported by four exposed stone arches. The outer sidewalls and the curved rear wall were not plastered, and the artistic stone masonry may be clearly seen.

Behind the rear chapel wall, in the *camposanto,* lie numerous stone-covered graves and a few elaborate tombs. There are no markings to allow the visitor to identify the names of the deceased, but surely they rest in peace in this place of beauty and isolation.

In 1768, the Indian population totaled nearly 800 at *San Luis Gonzaga* and nearby *Dolores Chillá,* when Visitador-General Gálvez ordered that these missions be closed and their charges moved to *Misión Santa Rosa de las Palmas*, near Todos Santos, 120 miles southeastward on the Pacific. As *San Luis Gonzaga* was never self-sustaining, the difficulty of importing food from the mainland forced this drastic and unpopular decision.

Flanking the mission, the crumbling roofless colonial building, constructed of flat-fired brick, may have originally been used as housing for the priests, and then perhaps been modified

Left: *The skillfully crafted stonework features unique arched windows and a curved rear wall behind the altar. Note the interesting curve made by the intersection of the altar wall and the barrel-vaulted roof.*

Right: *The stone arches supporting the roof are clearly visible from the austere and elegantly simple interior. Cut stone tiles were used to pave the floor.*

Misión San Luis Gonzaga Chiriyaqui

to Colonial style and expanded for use as a ranch structure. Two stages of construction are discernable. The portion the farthest from the mission is made of long, nearly rectangular brick, while the portion adjacent to the church is of flat, crudely formed tile-shaped brick.

In 1769, after the missionaries departed, an ex-mission soldier, Félix Romero, was granted the mission and all of its lands. However, he soon left *San Luis Gonzaga* and returned to La Paz. The grant then passed to Pablo de la Toba, who with his family operated a large cattle ranch on the old mission lands for many years.

Across the roadway from the church, a large colonnaded building of adobe and bricks, probably built in the late 1800s, stands empty; this building was reportedly headquarters for the ranch when it was operated by the de la Toba family.

A dam crosses the watercourse that flows parallel to the mission facade, about 400 yards distant. At its highest point the dam is less than 6 feet—however, it is several hundred yards long and hence could store a large amount of water. Rock-lined *acequias* developed by the missionaries allowed cultivation of the usual mission crops, including dates, sugarcane, and, of course, grapes, in the nearby irrigated fields.

The beautiful dam was made of the same rose-colored stone used for the chapel. Apparently the dam was breached by a past torrent and the gap partially filled with palm logs.

Misión San Luis Gonzaga Chiriyaqui

The *arroyo*, which is only 15 or 20 feet below the level of the plaza, is beautifully lined with palms and reeds and provides a welcome patch of green in this hot flat area on the rim of the Magdalena Plain.

Several families live between the mission and the watercourse in thatch-roofed houses. A small elementary school and a playground nearby serve the children of the village and those of the ranches in the area. Basic necessities are available at the government store, and a house of concrete block for the schoolmaster and his wife complete this tiny community.

Even though the main door to the church hung askew by one hinge, the interior, with rectangular-cut stone tiles paving the floor, was clean and in good condition during our visit in the fall of 1997.

The mission is easily accessible from Highway 1 by making a turn to the east 10 miles south of Ciudad Constitución. Then a 23-mile drive over reasonable dirt roads through interesting desert terrain takes the traveler back 250 years to this well-preserved and fascinating site.

Above right: *Thatched homes are located on the arroyo bank overlooking a sometimes wet pond. Next to the houses, the stone flank of the dam can be seen.*

Right: *The camposanto is enclosed by a nicely made stone wall and contains a dozen or so graves, a few of them elaborate stone-and-brick tombs.*

Misión San Luis Gonzaga Chiriyaqui

This deteriorating ruin, a few hundred yards from the church, contains stone-and-mortar mission-type walls, as well as flat adobe-like brick, supplemented with more recently applied rectangular red brick wall segments.

1740 – 1780*

Visita San Pablo

FOUNDED BY FATHER FERNANDO CONSAG, S.J.

N 27° 48.50'   W 113° 15.10' **

* EXACT ABANDONMENT DATE UNKNOWN
** ESTIMATED—NOT G.P.S. DATA

Visita San Pablo

MCDONALD, 1950

Visita San Pablo is located in the canyon of San Pablo, which is best known for its cave paintings and rock art.

Visita San Pablo

If you are looking for the fabled and mysterious "lost mission of Baja California," the often misnamed and little known adobe ruins deep in the Sierra San Francisco would be a fascinating discovery.

Even now, more than 250 years after its founding, this fallen chapel is accessible only by foot or pack animal. Few people other than backcountry ranchers and adventurous patrons of rock art make their way into this remote canyon.

Visita San Pablo was established by Father Fernando Consag of *Misión San Ignacio* in about 1740. Consag discovered the site and its numerous Indians during one of his frequent exploratory probes about the peninsula.

The ruins are located in the canyon of San Pablo, nearly 40 miles north of *San Ignacio* and 20 miles south of *Santa Gertrudis*. As *Santa Gertrudis* was developed as a *visita* of *Misión San Ignacio* early in the 1740s, it is likely that *San Pablo* was established during the same era as a way station between *San Ignacio* and *Santa Gertrudis*, and serviced periodically by the priests from *San Ignacio*.

Some writers have called *Visita San Pablo,* "Dolores del Norte," and to further confuse the correct names of these establishments, what is now called *Misíon Santa Gertrudis* was described as "Dolores del Norte" in a report dated 1745 by a Jesuit historian. Also, Father Zephyrin Englehardt, author of the detailed historical tomes, *Missions and Missionaries of California,* sometimes calls *Santa Gertrudis,* "Dolores del Norte."

In any event, the adobe ruins in the canyon of San Pablo mark what was certainly a Jesuit visiting station. This area and the surrounding mountains have become well-known for the large figures of humans and animals that decorate the caves under the overhanging walls of the canyon. This rich black-and-red rock art, remnant of an early civilization, is carefully described and illustrated in Crosby's publication, *The Cave Paintings of Baja California.*

Marquis McDonald and Glen Oster made a side trip on muleback to visit the site on their 1949–1950 Jeep exploration traversing the length of Baja California. They photographed the structure and reported it to be of adobe and arranged as "one long building separated into three rooms." Crosby estimated the size of the building as 130 feet long and 21 feet wide. He further states that "south of the church is a massive stone corral," and that the remains of a large *huerta* and irrigation system are visible on the opposite side of the canyon.

The fate of this *visita*—disease, decline of population, and finally abandonment—is clear. However, the usual data provided by the meticulous Jesuits—births, marriages, deaths, baptisms, and an inventory of possessions—seems not to have survived. *San Pablo* almost surely functioned into the Dominican era, but the Dominican records also are not available to indicate the statistics regarding the decline of this remote visiting station and its native population.

Irreparable damage has been wrought on the missions by fools digging in walls and floors searching for hidden treasures. Certainly, the only treasures the impoverished padres found here were the souls of the Indian converts.

Visita San Pablo

CROSBY

This intriguing rock art, located in the canyon of San Pablo, may be visited by hiring a guide at Rancho San Francisco, 35 miles north of San Ignacio.

1741 – 1768

Misión Nuestra Señora de los Dolores Chillá
Visita la Pasión

REFOUNDED BY FATHER LAMBERTO HOSTELL, S.J.

N 24° 53.280'   W 111° 01.878'

Misión Nuestra Señora de los Dolores Chillá

This wall section, which was still standing at the last site of the mission in 1967, is now reduced to a heap of stone rubble.

Misión Nuestra Señora de los Dolores Chillá

The area of the final location of *Misión Nuestra Señora de los Dolores,* called *Chillá* by the native *Guaycura,* lies in a shallow *arroyo* on a mountain plain more than 1,000 feet above sea level and 20 miles southwest of Father Guillén's original gulfside canyon site *(Apaté).*

A *visita* of *Misión Dolores Apaté* called *La Pasión* had been located at *Chillá.* It was later used as the new headquarters for the mission when it was reestablished by Father Lamberto Hostell in 1741.

In spite of the extensive development of the first site at the gulf, lack of consistent water and the torturous climb out of the canyon to communicate with the other missions caused the abandonment of the gulfside facilities. The mission was relocated to a more convenient and better watered area in the mountain arroyo that had been previously used for the visita.

Misión Dolores Chillá was soon reduced to a visita of *Misión San Luis Gonzaga,* 20 miles to the west, and continued to function until it was closed in 1768 by order of the king's emissary, the powerful Visitador-General José de Gálvez.

A goat ranch lies next to the fallen and deteriorating remnants of the largest mission building. The mound of stones is nearly 120 feet long and 40 feet wide.

Note: Early writers and current historians describe *Dolores* as having moved 10 leagues from gulfside *Apaté* to a site called *Tañuetía—Place of the ducks,* in 1733, 1737, and 1741. Crosby indicates that a move planned in 1734 was delayed until 1741 because of the Indian rebellion at the four southern missions. *Tañuetía* is perhaps a specific location within the area called *Chillá.*

Misión Nuestra Señora de los Dolores Chillá

111° 01.878' W

24° 53.280' N

24° 53.280' N

**Visita
La Pasión**

Misión Dolores Chillá
(3rd site)

Acequia

Arroyo La Presa

Road

Pila
(Reservoir)

Stone
Wall

Huerta
(Mission
Garden)

**Rancho
La Presa**

Dam
Remnants

The masonry columns supporting the roof over the front porch at Rancho La Presa are deteriorating but beautifully detailed.

N

| 0 | 1/8 | 1/4 | 3/8 | 1/2 mi. |

scale

The "boulder" in the foreground is composed of local stones bound with mortar. This is the largest remnant of what must have been the main mission building that was, perhaps, destroyed by an earthquake or other natural disaster.

111° 01.878' W

Edward Vernon, Santa Barbara, CA (805) 969-4123

©2002 Maps.com, Santa Barbara, CA (800) 929-4MAP   www.maps.com

Misión Nuestra Señora de los Dolores Chillá

The carefully made pila, 60 by 50 feet, receives water from a 1½-mile-long acequia that originates in the canyon bottom just below the mission site. Quarried stone and mortar were used to build the reservoir, and its interior is plastered.

Still in use when sufficient water is available, this acequia has conducted water to the fields of Rancho La Presa since the mission days.

The ruins of *La Pasión* are about one-quarter mile from the arroyo bed on a typical bench between the stream and the rising canyon walls. In 1998, the largest remnants of the mission were a T-shaped rock pile, approximately 120 feet long by 60 feet wide. The length of the mission building aligns almost directly north and south. Only one large "boulder" of stone and mortar and a long heap of rocks, some with mortar still clinging to their surfaces, are evident. No typical mission tile sherds were seen, which probably indicates that neither tile flooring nor roofing was used.

Misión Nuestra Señora de los Dolores Chillá

The ruins, a rock heap 2 to 3 feet high, currently border the grazing place for a herd of goats, the property of an adjacent *rancho* populated by the family of Señor Máximo Amador. About 200 feet southeast of the principal ruins and behind a goat pen are additional stone foundation traces measuring 40 by 50 feet. Perhaps these indicate the former location of some sort of housing or storeroom.

Downstream of the mission ruins a few hundred yards, the road crosses an *acequia* that turns and parallels the road on the opposite side of the arroyo and terminates 1½ miles downstream in a beautiful stone *pila*. The pila, built on the west side of Arroyo La Presa, as the canyon is now called, is of carefully laid stone with well-made bastions on the east and south walls. The west and north walls are backed by the rising slope of the canyon. The acequia continues from the lower end of the pila (where a modern iron gate valve has been installed) along the side of a large field that looks to have been a former mission garden.

Above right: *The newly established garden in front of the very old rancho building uses water pumped from the streambed behind the nearby winery to supplement water supplied by the acequia/pila system.*

Right: *The stone-and-mortar constuction is clearly shown at the unplastered end of the building. Note also the carved stone flame on the corner and the details that are reminiscent of Jesuit churches.*

Misión Nuestra Señora de los Dolores Chillá

The *huerta* is 200 yards wide, 3/4 mile long, and perfectly flat. The acequia and a volcanic incline form the west side of the huerta. The east side, which drops off to Arroyo La Presa, is bordered by a wall of round volcanic and river stones laid without mortar. Near the south end, one encounters the beautiful old home of Rancho La Presa, said to be "muy viejo."

The ranch house is constructed of stone and mortar. The tile roof described by McDonald in 1950 has been replaced by plywood and roll roofing. Long covered porches are attached to the front and back of the structure, and the four corners of the house are each accented by a large stone torch sculpture, typical of Jesuit churches. Twenty yards or so from the rear of house is the nearly intact stone-and-mortar facade, probably built during the same era of what is locally thought to be the ruins of a winery or storeroom.

The ranch house and winery stand on a flat above a lush, palm-filled bend in Arroyo La Presa. Locally it is stated that water has always been available from the watercourse, and this is confirmed by the apparent lack of a well near the ranch house. Depending on the literature that is read, this *rancho* is identified as Rancho La Presa or Rancho San Pedro,

Only this sturdy and interesting facade remains from what is thought to be a mission-era winery. The brick oven seen through the arched doorway probably was of later construction, and may have been used for the baking of bread or refining of sugarcane.

Misión Nuestra Señora de los Dolores Chillá

Señor Juan de Oios Espinosa, who lives nearby, is helping the new American owners of Rancho La Presa deal with the rigors of Baja California farming.

This huerta, irrigated from the stone pila, is perfectly flat and bordered by a dry-laid stone wall. From appearances, crops have not been raised on this land for several years. Records show, however, that a surprising variety of fruit and vegetables were raised from the gardens of the mission.

and in 1999 was occupied by an American couple with two young children.

The area was extensively developed by the padres and included a stone dam spanning the streambed one mile downstream from the ranch house. This dam must have provided water to the terrain below for either farming or grazing. Some

of the development in the surrounding countryside could have been made after the mission era.

One historian thinks that Rancho La Presa was built in the Jesuit era and first used as headquarters for a mission ranch. After the closing of *San Luis Gonzaga* and *Dolores* by Visitador-General Gálvez, some say the ranch house served as a chapel.

Misión Nuestra Señora de los Dolores Chillá

Sections of the dam of stone and mortar still cling to the solid rock river bed. The span of nearly 100 yards has been fragmented by floodwaters from past torrential downpours. The dam may have been part of the water system developed during the active days of the mission.

Englehardt expresses very well the missions' 1768 "extinction" when he writes, "Accordingly the missions of Dolores and San Luis Gonzaga…were abandoned, and their eight hundred people, accompanied by their missionaries, made their homes in Todos Santos, where good land and water abounded. Its own few Indians were sent to Mission Santiago, where Gálvez intended to organize the natives into a pueblo." Englehardt goes on to say, "the decrees were executed…by Ayudante Mayor Juan Gutiérrez, and…by José Garaza, lieutenant of the dragoons, each having a number of soldiers to aid him." Not only were decades of work and development by the padres abandoned, but the Indians were forced to move from the lands that had been their home for centuries!

The two abandoned missions were then used as way stations on the long expanse of El Camino Real between La Paz and San Javier. Later an ex-mission soldier named Félix Romero was given the land, but soon sold it to the de la Toba family of La Paz, who further developed the property and raised cattle on the old mission lands for many years. Now only a few scattered ranches populate this vast and lonely territory.

Misión Nuestra Señora de los Dolores Chillá

Water is always found at this oasis by a sharp bend in Arroyo La Presa. The ranch house sits on a bench 50 feet above the creek bottom. Could this beautiful spot of perennial water and greenery have been Tañuetía—the Place of the ducks, mentioned as one of the last sites of the mission?

1751 – 1822

Misión Santa Gertrudis
de Cadacamán

FOUNDED BY FATHER JORGE RETZ, S.J.

N 28º 03.085´   W 113º 05.083´

Misión Santa Gertrudis de Cadacamán

VERNON, 1997

Misión Santa Gertrudis in 1997 after extensive recent restoration.

Misión Santa Gertrudis de Cadacamán

Misión Santa Gertrudis, founded in 1751 by the German Jesuit Father Jorge Retz, is located 50 miles east of Guerrero Negro (and the famed Scammon's Lagoon), in low mountains east of the Vizcaíno desert near the almost deserted mining town of El Arco. The site, 50 miles north of *Misión San Ignacio*, was discovered by the great explorer Father Fernando Consag, who converted many Indians and commenced building facilities at the green oasis a year prior to the formal founding of the mission.

Misión Santa Gertrudis was called *Dolores del Norte* by some historians, as was the *visita* halfway between *Santa Gertrudis* and *San Ignacio*. The visita of *Misión San Ignacio* might better be called *San Pablo,* and still stands in the canyon of San Pablo just north of the present-day mountain *rancho,* San Francisco, a well-known base for expeditions for rock-art viewing.

Nestled against the steep mountain backdrop, *Santa Gertrudis* stands above an *arroyo* on a flood plain, elevated about 50 feet above the creek bed. The surrounding terrain is very rugged—the rock- and lava-strewn hills are heavily populated by many cactus varieties, including the giant cardon. The banks of the palm-lined and usually flowing stream are the home of several small ranches whose tenants raise livestock and cultivate small garden plots on what must have been mission *huertas.*

Three old mission bells hang in the stone tower, which faces the courtyard in front of the church. This picture was taken from the arroyo behind the tower.

Misión Santa Gertrudis de Cadacamán

Made of cut stone, the mission was extensively remodeled in 1977 and is in excellent shape. Missing or deteriorating stones on the exterior corners have been replaced and the roof strengthened. The main entry and the four windows on the front of the building have been rebuilt with stone trim similar to the original. The window nearest the altar end of the facade was created from what old photographs show as a doorway. New front steps and walks have greatly improved the appearance and approach to the main entry; the interior of the church and adjoining museum have been freshly plastered. A chain-link fence surrounds the buildings, adding to the security but not to the appearance of the site.

The altar has been redone in an ornate classic design, including marble fluted columns, replacing the very plain and simple original configuration shown by photographs taken 40 or 50 years ago. Sadly, the remodeling has erased the authentic time-worn look acquired by 245 years of aging—nevertheless, the structure is now in much better physical condition and will be preserved for services and viewing for many more years.

The mission is not as much a handsome architectural work as it is simply a long, towerless, rectangular building with little exterior adornment except some carved stonework surrounding the main entry on the north face. It is, however, most interesting

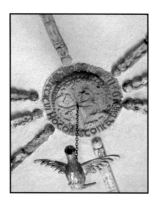

A baptismal font stands just inside the main entry, which has been beautifully reconstructed and accurately matches the weathered original portal, shown on the facing page. A carved bird hangs from the nicely restored and detailed ceiling of the museum.

Arthur North's 1905 photo was captioned, "The aged Cochimí of Santa Gertrudis."

The mission's condition had apparently changed little between 1905 and 1960, the date of this photo by Michael Mathes.

because of its history, antiquity, and location in a remote ranching community. The extensive collection of mission artifacts in the small museum abutting the chapel displays fascinating remnants of the lives of the missionaries and their converts.

During the restoration, the foundation of an earlier structure, probably built of adobe, was encountered 50 yards from the stone chapel. This foundation, running perpendicular to the chapel face, is over 3 feet wide and composed of stones that were set into a deep trench in the earth. A section has been uncovered, fenced, and labeled for visitor viewing.

Misión Santa Gertrudis is unique in that it is the only Baja California mission that has a separate bell tower. This stone tower with three bells stands gracefully on the brow of the slope to the creek beside the plaza in front of the church.

Paralleling the creek, an *acequia* still in use leads from over one mile upstream past the bell tower to provide water to the gardens of the few small ranch houses a few hundred yards downstream from the mission. During the days of the mission's operation, the acequia furnished water to the fields that were expanded for farming purposes by soil that had been packed in on muleback. As much of that soil has been washed away by infrequent but torrential Baja storms, only small plots remain for gardens. Reports indicate that a wide variety of vegetables and fruit, including corn, dates, olives, and figs, was produced from these fields while being cultivated by the missionaries.

An interesting account of mission life, written by Father Junípero Serra during his 1769 inspection of the missions newly under the charge of the Franciscan order, revealed that Father Dionisio Basterra, the priest at *Santa Gertrudis*, proudly greeted the famous

El Camino Real heads northward toward Mission San Borja. This "Royal Highway," designed for pack mules and foot traffic, is clearly visible and still in use today.

A trough hewn from a single piece of stone was probably a wine vat. Note that the upper edge has been notched to receive planks that were sealed in place with pitch.

Father Serra on his arrival with a great ceremony, including a parade, singing by the Christian Indians, and, of course, a special mass. On completion of the formal ceremony, the two men met privately and Father Basterra, with tears in his eyes, told Father Serra of his terrible loneliness. His only soldier and his servant had been removed for other duties, leaving the devout padre without an interpreter, alone with

Misión Santa Gertrudis de Cadacamán

Far left: *The redesigned and completely remodeled altar had just been completed in November 1997, when this photo was taken.*

Left: *Father Mario proudly displays the crucifix used to adorn the new altar of the mission church.*

the Indians, and barely able to function day by day because of a lack of communication and severe depression. Padre Serra was unable to promise relief and could only urge the man to carry on his priestly duties.

In 1762, there were more than 1,700 Indians being ministered to by *Misión Santa Gertrudis*. Because of the isolation, few of the European-bred epidemics had touched this area in its first years. However, eventually the devastating European diseases took hold and reduced the mission to fewer than 300 people by 1785. Only about 100 natives were left when the mission was abandoned in 1822.

In more recent times, *Santa Gertrudis* has served the local ranching community as a peaceful retreat and as a place of worship. Even though the lack of a permanent priest makes regular services impractical, frequent visits are made by clergy from surrounding communities to hold mass whenever possible.

The remodeling completed in 1997 was supervised by Father Mario Menghini Pecci with assistance from the engineering staff of the large salt mining company. Although their efforts have destroyed the original simplicity of this ancient mission, the structural improvements will ensure that the mission will stand for the contemplation of future generations.

Misión Santa Gertrudis de Cadacamán

The acequia winds down the canyon just below the mission from its water source nearly one mile upstream.

1762 – 1818

Misión San Francisco de Borja Adac

FOUNDED BY FATHER WENCESLAUS LINCK, S.J.

N 28° 45.104'   W 110° 03.552'

Misión San Francisco de Borja Adac

Located mid-peninsula between Bahía de los Angeles and the village of Rosarito, Misión San Borja is a striking example of the Baja California missions.

Misión San Francisco de Borja Adac

Left: *Looking toward the doorway from the dim central aisle of the church, the entry detail and the baptismal font are silhouetted against the bright desert sunlight.*

Right: *The chapel interior has a vaulted ceiling supported by five stone arches. Note the flattening of the arch nearest the altar.*

At the foot of a steep, lava-strewn hillside, springs surrounded by lush greenery formed a place called *Adac* by the native *Cochimí*. A chapel and simple irrigation system were built here by Father Jorge Retz in 1759, to serve as a *visita* for *Misión Santa Gertrudis* and to provide a base for the feeding and conversion of the many Indians living in *rancherías* in the area.

An endowment from a wealthy Italian noblewoman, María de Borja, funded the foundation and building of *Misión San Francisco de Borja* at the visita site by the Bohemian Jesuit priest Wenceslaus Linck, in 1762.

Misión San Francisco de Borja Adac

From the roof of the main structure, the mill building (molina) at the far corner of the courtyard may be seen.

A cowboy herds cattle on the same lands tended by his ancestors.

An adobe church, a hospital, living quarters, and storerooms were constructed by the Jesuits prior to the building of the existing stone church, which was completed in 1801 by the Dominicans. Behind the standing church are the nearly intact stone-and-mortar remains of a mill building, a winery, and a courtyard enclosed by high walls. The extensive adobe ruins of the earlier mission complex cover a large area behind the later-dated stone structures.

The low, rectangular, towerless church is in remarkably good condition. Only a minimum amount of restoration was necessary to rebuild the upper part of the square, truncated bell tower. The stone, barrel-vaulted roof covering the nave and altar was made in five sections. Hopefully, the concrete cap added to the roof, accomplished during the restoration, will prevent the flattening ceiling arch near the altar from collapsing.

The entry facade is one of the most beautiful of all the missions. The detailed, heavily ornamented design stands out in strong contrast to the otherwise rather plain exterior.

The mission buildings are beautifully crafted from local stone cut into rectangular blocks. Doorways and windows are surrounded by intricate designs carved in stone. One of the side doors features open lattice work in a sunrise design in the arched overhead, as does the main entry portal, whose wood has probably been replaced many times. Lumber for the original doors must have been brought from Mexico (or Spain), as there was virtually no suitable timber for grand mission entrances growing in Baja California.

Another side door, rectangular in shape, is also decorated by hand-carved stone ornamentation. The patterns on each side and above the door must have

Originally a pair of heavy paneled doors must have filled this impressive entryway. The recently installed angled siding and too-small door secure the building but are not esthetically pleasing.

This skillfully carved ornamental window overlooks the courtyard, bordered by the winery and mill buildings.

Misión San Francisco de Borja Adac

religious significance. The worn stone sill makes it easy to imagine the many faithful neophytes who must have passed through this portal to hear a devout padre say mass.

Inside the church, a circular staircase leading from the vestibule gives access to the truncated (or perhaps never completed) bell tower, the choir loft, and the roof of the mission. Each musical note-shaped step is cut from a single stone. The circular keys are stacked atop each other and doweled at their center, with each staff rotated appropriately to form a step. The well-like stone casing of the stairway was evidently laid up in the same sequence as the steps. Each step's outer end is embedded into a matching course of the casing. Climb with caution, as each step is only 8 inches wide at the circumference and tapers to 3 inches at the center.

The mission faces up a wide canyon, enclosed on two sides by high plateaus created by age-old volcanic flows. A usually dry creek bed winds down the canyon past the mission to spread out across the sandy, rocky desert floor. Several hot springs emerge in small rock-lined pools. These and nearby cold springs sustained the plant and animal life that attracted the *Cochimí* rancherías and the missionaries to inhabit the area.

Extensive water storage and distribution systems were built during the development of the mission to enable the growing of crops to feed the missionaries, soldiers, servants, and the many newly dependent converts. Rock-lined ditches were constructed to direct the water to flow from the springs to stone reservoirs called *pilas,* which had several gates to allow water to be diverted to a particular field.

Above left: *The individual musical note-shaped steps, fitted into a casing 3 feet in diameter, are shown from the top of the stairway.*

Left: *A single block of stone was used to carve this elaborate baptismal font.*

Misión San Francisco de Borja Adac

An adobe wall of the first mission ends at a stone building marked "molina/mill" by a newly placed sign.

Adobe ruins of the surprisingly large initial mission that was commenced about 1762 are shown by this view from the roof of the 1801 stone church.

The mission water system is in use today to irrigate the same fields that helped to sustain the padres and their neophytes. The resident local family grows beans, corn, grapes, citrus, and other fruit and vegetables.

Wine produced at the mission was stored in large tubs carved from a single stone, then covered with a flat rock or boards and sealed with pitch. Water troughs for the livestock, also cut from a single stone, are still in use today.

To the east, a mesa with spring water was used by the missionaries to graze over 600 head of cattle. During a recent

Misión San Francisco de Borja Adac

The brother of the girls to the right shows the hot spring that drains into a stone pila below, where water is stored for irrigation. The water is quite "fragrant" but supposedly becomes drinkable after standing and cooling. A close-by cold spring is piped to the ranch house between the spring and the mission church.

These cute niñas, the children of the mission caretakers, are standing on the roof of the church that overlooks the adobe ruins of the first mission.

visit, a local *vaquero,* clad in thick leather chaps and astride a white mule, was asked the size of his herd. He replied, "Seiscientos, más o menos"—the same number of animals as supported by the land in the mission days!

In spite of the agricultural activity, this mission was not self-sustaining, and it was necessary to import supplies from the mainland by ship via Loreto. Los Angeles Bay, about 15 miles to the northeast, served as the nearest supply port.

At the peak of *San Borja's* activities, in 1765, 59 Indian families, a total of 268 *almas* (souls), lived on the mission grounds. The area of influence of the church also included an additional 3,000 natives in five surrounding rancherías, spread over an area of approximately 3,600 square miles. However, by 1800, the perennial curse of imported disease decimated the population; at this time, fewer than 400 Indians were left throughout the area. By 1818, so few natives were living that the mission was abandoned.

Misión San Borja is a delightful place to visit to see the well-preserved buildings and extensive mission complex. The caretaker family is gracious and proud to show the mission and its grounds to visitors. Also, there are several fascinating cave painting sites in the vicinity that may be visited with the aid of a local guide.

Above right: *The green field lies in the canyon bottom just a few hundred yards upstream from the stone church. The beautiful garden of fruit and vegetables is watered by the original mission system.*

Right: *Fed by hillside springs, this pila stores water for the irrigation of the crops through a system of canals leading to the fields below.*

Misión San Francisco de Borja Adac

This photograph by Michael Mathes shows the original bells and the condition of the mission in 1960 before several refurbishments. The left corner of the tower has since been rebuilt.

1766 – 1767

Visita de Calamajué*

FOUNDED BY FATHERS VICTORIANO ARNÉS, S.J. & JUAN DÍEZ, S.J

N 29° 25.255'   W 114° 11.698'

*ATTEMPTED FIRST SITE FOR MISIÓN SANTA MARÍA

These 15 by 90-foot ruins of what are probably the remnants of the chapel, sacristy, and storeroom, are the largest building footprint on the site.

Visita de Calamajué

alamajué was the Indian place-name for what was to become the first site of *Misión Santa María de los Angeles*. Jesuit Fathers Victoriano Arnés and Juan José Díez, with a party including 10 soldiers and 50 neophyte Indians from *Misión San Borja,* established a short-lived mission here in October 1766.

The location, 55 miles north of *Misión San Borja,* had been discovered by Father Consag in 1751 while searching the gulf coast for a new mission site. *Calamajué* was again visited by Father Linck early in 1766 during his exploration, which ventured northward as far as the rugged slopes of the San Pedro Mártir range, some 60 miles farther north.

Above right: *The broad river bottom, 150 feet below the bench of the mission ruins, is covered with coarse grass, which probably led the mission founders into believing the land was arable. The high mineral content in the water will not support crops and is likely to cause man and beast considerable anguish.*

Right: *McDonald took this photo in 1951, and it appears that the slump of the standing wall of the chapel was about 5 feet high at that time.*

Visita de Calamajué

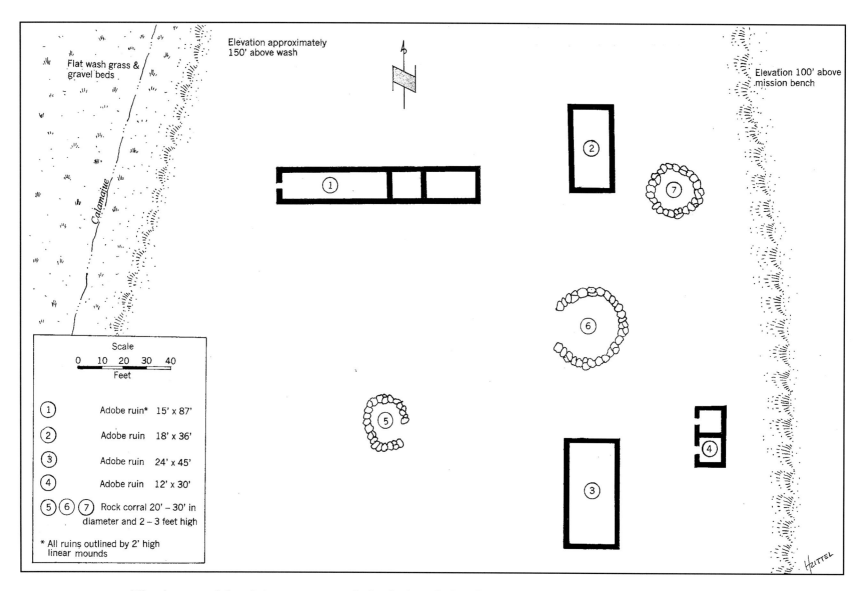

Elevation approximately 150' above wash

Flat wash grass & gravel beds

Calamajué

Elevation 100' above mission bench

Scale
0 10 20 30 40
Feet

①   Adobe ruin*   15' x 87'

②   Adobe ruin   18' x 36'

③   Adobe ruin   24' x 45'

④   Adobe ruin   12' x 30'

⑤ ⑥ ⑦   Rock corral 20' – 30' in diameter and 2 – 3 feet high

* All ruins outlined by 2' high linear mounds

The placement of the mission remnants on the bench above the broad, flat wash is shown by this field sketch made in 1999.

Visita de Calamajué

Shortly after commencing work at the site, Father Díez became ill and was forced to return to *San Borja* for care. Father Arnés continued to operate the struggling encampment under very difficult circumstances. Not only was food scarce, but a rebellion by the surrounding Indians required help from the faithful Indians of *San Borja* to subdue.

Even though there were many Indians available for conversion, and easy access to the gulf, the site quickly proved unsuccessful. The moist grassy flat below the buildings was so laden with salts that all attempts to cultivate wheat and other crops failed. However, it is remarkable that in the seven-month life of the "mission," roads and trails were cleared and many buildings erected.

During its short life, it is not clear whether *Calamajué* actually had the status of a mission or served only as a *visita*. Nevertheless, the melted remnants of this compound are interesting reminders of the Jesuits' determination to reach every possible location, populated by natives who required the padres' services for the salvation of their souls.

The rock corral, 20 feet in diameter, was laid without mortar, and must have been in use during the days this site served as a way station for pack trains between San Borja and Santa María.

After the closing of the mission, Father Arnés went 30 miles northward, to a place called *Cabujakaamung* by the Indians, to again attempt to found *Misión Santa María. Calamajué* then served as a visiting station, shelter, and a way station for pack trains between *San Borja, Santa María,* and *Velicatá.*

Building remnants at the site include the outline of four adobe structures marked by linear mounds 2 to 3 feet high. The largest adobe ruin, 90 feet long by 15 feet

This creek flows almost due north down the scenic Arroyo Calamajué toward the Sea of Cortés. The canyon widens near the site of the mission, where the flow of water disappears into the sandy soil.

wide, is divided into three sections. The principal room, probably the chapel, is 15 by 48 feet, with the narrow entry end facing west across the half-mile-wide grass-covered river bottom. The other rooms, to the rear, probably served as sacristy and storeroom. The chapel, with its facade on the rim of the bench 150 feet above the riverbed, must have appeared quite dramatic.

Three other ruined adobe structure remnants are located nearby on the 1,000 by 300-foot flat above the riverbed. The dimensions of a one-room outbuilding measure 18 by 36 feet. The second separate single room ruin is 24 by 45 feet, and the third, remnants of a two-room structure, is 12 by 30 feet. All of these former structures are marked only by outlines made of melted adobe mounds. If excavation could be done, it would be typical to find wide stone foundations under the center line of each mound.

Scattered on the flat site among the rocks and cactus are three round or oval enclosures with dry-laid rock walls 3 to 5 feet in height; the largest is 30 feet in diameter. These enclosures were perhaps used as corrals.

A distinct rock-bordered trace, probably originally an Indian trail and what is left of this portion of El Camino Real, leaves the perimeter of the compound heading south in the general direction of *Misión San Borja.*

Many years after the end of the mission era, numerous small mining operations were undertaken on the peninsula. Gold or silver was mined directly opposite the mission site across the riverbed on the west bank of the arroyo. The site of the ore mill is marked by large stone foundations on the crest of the bluff. A horizontal shaft penetrates the 150-foot-high vertical riverbank below the mill foundations. This mine probably was active sometime between 1890 and 1920 while attempts to commercialize mining were at their highest in this region.

Ruins of a long-deserted mining and milling operation stand on the west bank of the wide sandy canyon Calamajué, directly opposite the mission location.

Visita de Calamajué

This trail was probably originally used by the Indians of the area and later carried the pack trains that traversed the peninsula between San Borja and Santa María.

1767 – 1769

Misión Santa María de los Angeles

Cabujakaamung

FOUNDED BY FATHER VICTORIANO ARNÉS, S.J.

N 29° 43.888' W 114° 32.821'

Misión Santa María de los Angeles Cabujakaamung

The chapel ruins lie on a flat bench above a palm-lined perennial creek. The still-standing gable ends testify to the dry climate and remote location.

Misión Santa María de los Angeles Cabujakaamung

The last of the missions founded by the Jesuits, *Santa María* was established in a narrow, rocky canyon bottom to replace *Visita de Calamajué*, which had been put in an even less hospitable location. In 1767, Father Victoriano Arnés selected this *arroyo* with a small spring, called *Cabujakaamung* by the native *Cochimí* Indians. The mission was short-lived because of the scant water, little pasturage, and almost no land suitable for raising crops.

The first Spanish to visit the area were led by the explorer/priest Fernando Consag in 1751. Later, Father Linck of *Misión San Borja* passed through the same arroyo on a 1764 expedition to the nearby gulf island of Angel de la Guardia.

Father Arnés, who abandoned the unsatisfactory site at *Calamajué* to reestablish *Misión Santa María* at *Cabujakaamung*, had just begun to develop the area when he was forced, early in 1768, to return to Loreto in response to the order by King Carlos III of Spain expelling all Jesuits from the New World. Several months later, in May of the same year, the mission was again reestablished by Juan José Beitia, the new Franciscan priest assigned to this northernmost frontier mission outpost.

Above right: *The padre's casa, to the right of the chapel, is surprisingly complete in this 1951 photo by Marquis McDonald, in spite of being roofless for more than 100 years.*

Right: *The adobe walls next to the altar end of the mission are the remnants of the padre's casa and storeroom. The holes in the walls were probably cut by vandals searching for the ever tempting "lost treasures of the missions."*

Misión Santa María de los Angeles Cabujakaamung

C. VERNON

Using an endowment from the generous Doña María Borja, who also funded the building of *Misión San Borja,* an adobe church was built, approximately 30 by 90 feet, roofed with thatch and reeds. Another adobe structure of two rooms was constructed adjacent to the church, probably for use as a storeroom and dwelling. These buildings were erected by Father Beitia to replace the crude stick-and-brush structures initially placed at the site.

Supplies for the mission were brought in either by mule over an 80-mile trail from *San Borja,* or by ship from Loreto and the mainland. Pack animals then climbed a steep rocky 12-mile trail from Bahía San Luis Gonzaga, the nearest anchorage, in order to deliver goods to *Misión Santa María.*

In 1768, nearly 500 Indians living in the surrounding territory came under the influence of *Santa María.* However, only five families and a few single Indians were able to live at the mission because of the scarcity of water and the difficulties in growing crops.

Life at this mission was always precarious because of the ongoing necessity of importing food and supplies from Loreto. As these shipments were often delayed due to transportation difficulties or lack of resources, hunger drove many converts back to their primitive life of hunting and gathering.

The east-facing entry doorway still stands virtually intact more than 230 years after being built. The rear gable wall is also surprisingly well preserved, even though the roof disintegrated many years ago.

Misión Santa María de los Angeles Cabujakaamung

Santa María's most noteworthy role in the development of the California mission chain occurred in May 1768, when the well-known Franciscan priest, Father Junípero Serra, joined by Governor Gaspar de Portolá, proceeded up the peninsula to meet the overland expedition gathered at nearby *Velicatá*. The party then trekked 300 miles northward to aid in the founding of a new mission at San Diego.

Governor Portolá's troops had stopped earlier at *Santa María* but, because of the lack of pasturage for the considerable expedition and pack train, proceeded 50 miles northwest to await Father Serra at a grassy area known to the Indians as *Velicatá*. On joining Portolá's forces, Serra founded *Misión San Fernando Rey de España,* as the site offered reliable water, ample pasturage, and acres of flat land for the cultivation of crops.

Santa María was soon reduced to the status of a *visita* in 1769, administered by *San Borja*. In 1818, it was abandoned, but the buildings continued to serve as a way station for pack trains for a number of years.

The isolation of the locale and the almost negligible rainfall helped to preserve this interesting and historic site that marks the last of the Jesuit endeavours on the Baja California peninsula.

Above right: *The row of palms and grass line a small spring-fed creek that carries fresh, sweet water for a few hundred yards before it disappears into the sandy arroyo floor.*

Right: *Many rock corrals are found near the mission and in the side canyons close by.*

Misión Santa María de los Angeles Cabujakaamung

A difficult road leads 14 miles from Rancho Santa Inés to Santa María. It traverses interesting rock-strewn hills that support many cacti varieties, including Cholla, Pitahaya, and the curious Cirio.

1769 – 1818

Misión San Fernando Rey de España
de Velicatá

FOUNDED BY FATHER JUNÍPERO SERRA, O.F.M.

N 29° 58.319'   W 115° 14.180'

Misión San Fernando Rey de España de Velicatá

Only these few walls and mounds of melted adobe overlook the virtually deserted valley to mark the first and only Franciscan mission on the peninsula.

Misión San Fernando Rey de España de Velicatá

elicatá is the Indian name of a broad mid-peninsula valley 50 miles west of *Misión Santa María,* the northernmost Jesuit mission. The site had been discovered in 1766 by Father Wenceslaus Linck of *Misión San Borja* during an exploratory expedition that probed as far north as the future site of *Misión Santa Domingo.* It was here that Father Junípero Serra joined with the overland expedition led by Governor Gaspar de Portolá to venture north to San Diego to establish the first Alta California mission.

Portolá was drawn to the valley because of the available water and ample pasturage for his mounted expeditionary force and their many pack animals. After observing the attractive site, encountering the numerous unconverted natives, and realizing that a way station would be needed to aid in the communication with the future missions far to the north, Father Serra decided to found a mission at *Velicatá.* On May 14, 1769, a special mass was said to dedicate what was to be the first and only Franciscan mission in Baja California.

The ceremonies were held in an enclosure of standing sticks pounded into the ground with a roof of palm fronds

Above right: *There were substantial adobe ruins when this G. W. Hendry photograph was taken. Although the photo is undated, it appears to have been taken earlier than the time of the 1906 expedition of Arthur North.*

Right: *This photograph, taken by Michael Mathes in 1965, reveals the rapid deterioration of the building since the photo above.*

Misión San Fernando Rey de España de Velicatá

Arthur North captioned this 1905 photo, "The author and his party leaving the ruins of Junípero Serra's Mission of San Fernando de Velicatá."

and brush. Similar construction is used in many backcountry ranch buildings built and lived in today.

Serra left with Portolá on the 40-day trek to San Diego to fulfill his famous destiny in Alta California. He appointed Father Miguel de la Campa y Cos as the missionary in charge of the new establishment at *Velicatá*. Father Campa spent four years there, and is generally credited with the construction of the adobe church and other buildings at the complex.

Acequias about 30 feet above the sandy streambed follow the canyon walls to a *pila* about one mile downstream to the west. Meigs indicates that a stone-and-earth dam was located at springs near the mission, but no remnants were found dur-

ing recent trips to the site. In years with ample rain, several hundred acres of gardens could have been watered with the system, but as many floods have scoured the *arroyo* since the mission days, little evidence is left to delineate those areas.

The crops produced in the arroyo included wheat, corn, and barley—the soil was found to be too salty to produce fruit or vegetables. Cattle, sheep, and goats were grazed on the thousands of acres from the gulf to the Pacific that made up the mission lands.

During the Franciscan tenure, 1769 to 1773, nearly 500 baptisms were conducted and the population steadily increased, as the deadly European diseases had not yet taken root. At the

Misión San Fernando Rey de España de Velicatá

end of this period, the Dominicans took charge, and *San Fernando* was put under the leadership of Fathers Miguel Hidalgo and Pedro Gandiaga. The Franciscans were sent to Alta California to develop and Christianize that untouched land for the church and the King of Spain.

By 1776, the mission attained its largest population of about 1,400. This count probably encompassed the Indians in the huge territory—nearly 1,200 square miles—that came under the mission's jurisdiction. Also included were the converted natives who had lived in *rancherías* near the abandoned *Misión Santa María* and were brought under the control of the Dominicans at *Velicatá*. A number of *visitas* were established, including some that can be identified as *ranchos* today.

The rate of population increase reversed very quickly when an epidemic in the following year took the lives of one-third of the Indians. Attacks of smallpox and typhus further decimated them, some of whom had been infected with syphilis by the Spanish soldiers. The devastating effects of the epidemics and the dramatically reduced birth rate caused by syphilis had reduced the mission's population to 360 by the turn of the century.

Above left: *Looking south over the mission ruins, the cut in the far bank caused by flooding is apparent.*

Left: *The original stone foundations under the melted adobe walls have been exposed by recent excavation.*

Above: *An acequia that runs along the cliff toward the pila one mile downstream is being eroded by floods spreading from the streambed 15 feet below.*

Above right: *The face of the cliff is marked with numerous petroglyphs at eye level above the acequia.*

The records of baptisms and burials kept by the Dominicans end in 1821, although permanent residence by a priest probably ended about 1818. These records reveal that, from 1812 to 1822, only 19 baptisms were performed, while 58 burials were recorded. Only one birth (baptism) took place in the last seven years of record-keeping. A visitor in 1853 said that, "below the mission live four Indians, the youngest of which is over 70." As the Indian population faltered, the few survivors and their families moved to the mission village of El Rosario.

When the author visited in 1997, a single Mexican family resided in a nearby adobe and apparently subsisted by raising cattle and growing a small garden. They also earned a few *pesos* guiding visitors to the petroglyphs on the canyon wall

Misión San Fernando Rey de España de Velicatá

one-half mile downstream from the ruins. Two years later, the only person living on the site was Señor Candelario Acevedo Sainz, who claims that his family in Tiajuana holds title to the now virtually deserted old mission lands.

Not only is *Velicatá* fascinating because of its rich mission history, but the canyon walls carry the markings of far earlier inhabitants. Petroglyphs chipped into the desert varnish on the sheer, brown stone cliff on the north side of the arroyo picture complicated geometric designs, and what may be imagined to be human figures and war accoutrements.

During the flood of El Niño in late 1977, according to Señor Sainz, a torrent of water reaching from the north to the south canyon walls washed away any remaining evidence of mission gardens. Unfortunately this same torrent undermined the petroglyph-bearing cliff, and many markings disappeared when slabs of rock fell from the face.

In spite of the scant remnants, *Velicatá* is a wonderful place to visit and imagine the stirring scene of Captain Portolá and Father Serra meeting at this remote site. A few days later, leading their large mounted party of soldiers, Indians, and pack animals laden with supplies and mission furnishings, they departed for San Diego to establish the Spanish crown and the Catholic faith in what was destined to become California, U.S.A.

Is the figure standing on the pattern at the far right above intended to be a human male? To the left of that drawing, an imaginative swirl was made. Could the design to the lower right be a warshield? Is a man or a man/bird represented by the lower left design?

Water flowed to this pila through an acequia that approached from the mission dam one mile upstream and entered the pila at the narrow end to the left. The pila measures 75 by 40 feet and slopes to 6 feet in depth at the discharge end. Undoubtedly built in mission days, repairs by ranchers in the area have prevented deterioration.

1769 – 1817

Visita de la Presentación

FOUNDED BY FATHER FRANCISCO PALÓU, O.F.M.

N 23° 43.956' W 111° 32.575'

Visita de la Presentación

The chapel as it must have looked in the late 1700s.

Visita de la Presentación

De la Presentación was built as a visita for Misión San Javier in 1769 by the Franciscan priest, Francisco Palóu. Located almost exactly 10 miles due south of Misión San Javier, Visita de la Presentación stands on the east bank of the stream in Arroyo Santo Domingo. The canyon is quite narrow at this point and forms an almost flat floor between precipitous brush-covered walls capped by lava cliffs. Water flows most of the year, and as a result the canyon bottom is a dense, verdant strip of cactus, palms, and shrubs. This visita is an exciting place to find because it stands in a remote, rarely visited area, and includes more extensive ruins than are expected from the scant information available from the few Baja California missions texts that describe the site. The substantial remnants of its stone buildings and water system have survived more than 230 years since its erection.

The principal building measures 70 by 22 feet, with an interior of two rooms divided by a stone wall more than 10 feet high. An arched opening connects the two rooms. The front room, 14 by

The chapel was severely disintegrating when Michael Mathes took this photo in 1950—no wonder after 180 years!

36 feet, was probably the chapel. The 14 by 22-foot rear room could have been the sacristy or living quarters. The stones used for construction were selected (or cut) so that a flat surface would face the interior and facilitate plastering. Sand-and-cement mortar was used to lay-up all of the main building walls as well as for plastering the interior.

Visita de la Presentación

Above: *Arthur North's 1905 photo shows the carefully cut stones used to frame the chapel entry.*

Left: *By 1998, the doorway had deteriorated and been reduced to this diminished state.*

The visita's main entry on the east-facing short wall was beautifully crafted of accurately cut stones to form the door jambs and straight header anchored with a keystone. This wall creates a gable end, and it is presumed that the mission was covered by a simple palm-frond roof with a ridge that ran the length of the structure. As the roof of the chapel has disintegrated, the walls have progressively deteriorated from weather and from locals using the stones for home-building projects. The apex of the front wall is now approximately 12 feet high. It appears to be 16 or 18 feet high in a photograph taken over 50 years ago.

Visita de la Presentación

When standing on the barren compacted soil of the "plaza" area facing the visita's entry, a large corral may be seen 50 yards to the left. Its walls, made of rounded uncut stones laid without mortar, are approximately 5 feet high. The interior of the corral measures 60 by 60 feet. Most of the 4-foot-thick walls remain standing.

Above: *This doorway leads from the chapel to the smaller abutting room.*

Left: *Most of the plaster still adheres to the face of the interior dividing wall.*

To the right 50 feet, when facing the main entry, stand the remnants of another substantial stone building approximately 22 feet wide and 35 feet long. This building was also constructed of stone, but dry-laid without the use of mortar or plaster. In view of this simple construction, it is surprising that the sidewalls still stand more than 10 feet high. From examination of the ruins, it appears that the collapsed wall on the south (the narrow end of the structure) contained an exterior doorway. No other openings are evident.

The east- and west-facing sidewalls are nearly 12 feet high, and appear to be of their original height for a distance of about 20 feet in the center of the building. The end walls have collapsed, and it is assumed that these walls were built into gables to support the ridgepole of the roof. One account calls this structure a *troje* or granary.

Remnants of other small stone ruins, some of them circular, may

Visita de la Presentación

Above: *The brush-covered corral could still be used to hold livestock, and fronts one side of the "plaza" formed by the chapel and troje.*

Right: *One of the walls of the troje stands more than 18 feet high in spite of the lack of mortar bonding, and even supports the growth of a tenacious tree and shrubs.*

be found in the brush to the north of the visita. However, the best-preserved structure is the *pila,* which lies between the chapel and the river. The pila, which measures 70 by 70 feet, is 6 feet deep, and the top is at ground level. Cut stone steps descend at the center of each of the four walls to the floor. The steps on the north wall include an entry spillway for the water that must have been brought into the pila by an *acequia* from far-

ther up the river. The structure is perfectly square, and all sides and the bottom are plastered. Areas bare of plaster show that the pila was built of local rock as well as fired adobe blocks. The flat bottom is intact except that, at the precise center, several large stones have been removed to reveal a pit that was probably excavated by "treasure hunters" fantasizing over the padres' reputed hidden gold.

Visita de la Presentación

The chapel, corral, and outbuildings stand about 50 feet above and 300 yards east of the south-flowing stream. Halfway between these buildings and the creek is a large leveled area that appears to have been cultivated and probably served as the mission garden. The stream, lined with fan palms and shrubs, makes a delightful sight as it flows gently toward the south and then westward toward the shores of the Pacific Ocean.

Because of the fertility of the site, the ample water, and acreage available for agriculture, *Visita de la Presentación* was probably quite important in producing food for *Misión San Javier,* which helped provision *Loreto,* as little land or water was available at the mother mission and *presidio* to support agriculture. *Visita de la Presentación* was left to the elements in 1817 at a time when *Misión San Javier* was no longer able to sustain daily operations. Even this beautiful and productive spot was not spared the effects of diseases, which decimated the Indians and eventually forced abandonment of all the missions.

About one mile upstream from the site of *Visita de la Presentación,* an active *rancho* stands on what must have been mission lands. The walls are built of sticks driven into the ground and the roof is thatched with palm fronds—typical of backcountry construction in this area. Many goats roam the valley floor, and the rancho has a small garden, pigs, chickens, and a few flowers, as well as the ubiquitous pickup truck. Only a single family of goatherds remains at this fascinating site. What a contrast from the activity of the many Indians who must have labored on the visita's buildings, constructed the irrigation system, and tended crops during the development of the mission!

A graceful spillway flanked by stone steps leads from ground level down 6 feet to the stone bottom of the pila.

Visita de la Presentación

Palms and shrubs line this pretty creek hidden in the arroyo below the chapel grounds.

1774 – 1832

Misión Nuestra Señora del Rosario
de Viñadaco

FOUNDED BY FATHERS VICENTE MORA, O.P. & FRANCISCO GALISTEO, O.P.

*N 30° 02.485' W 115° 44.335'

* LOCATION OF 2ND SITE (ABAJO)

VERNON, 1997

The ruins of El Rosario de Abajo, the second mission site, still proudly display the only Gothic arched entry in all of the California missions.

Misión Nuestra Señora del Rosario de Viñadaco

Dominican Father-President Vicente Mora, in 1773, found an ideal location, just 35 miles west of the Franciscan mission at *Velicatá,* for the first of the nine Dominican missions to be established in Baja California. A wide, gently sloping valley, with easy access to the Pacific, offered a small stream of water and ample land for farming and grazing.

Mora had wells dug to uncover springs that flowed from the brown brush-dotted hills on the north side of the valley. A year later he established the mission between two small gullies on a fan one-half mile from the sandy, reed-filled river bottom and about 10 miles from the Pacific shore.

The foundation for the initial building was laid in 1774, and Father Francisco Galisteo was put in charge. By 1793, a church and sacristy, 25 by 125 feet, was in place, and by 1800, the large walled enclosure included housing for the priest and soldiers, a forge, a weaving room, storerooms, and separate cubicles for unmarried men and women neophytes. The main buildings were of adobe with

MEIGS, 1926

In 1926, many of the mission walls at the second site had not yet weathered away to mere mounds of adobe. Note the pieces of plaster clinging to various surfaces. A lime kiln must have been constructed to fire the limestone and shells necessary to make a crude cement to bind sand and water into plaster.

either palm-thatch or brush-and-mud roofs. Several guard towers were placed in the walls surrounding the mission, but proved unnecessary as natives in this area were quite adaptable to mission life.

A dam was erected across the gully beside the mission to capture water draining toward the river. The then ample flow came from a spring uncovered by Father Mora when he had his Indian followers dig an exploratory well during his first visit to the area.

Initially the mission was quite successful, as its location provided many acres of tillable land located on the bench just above the riverbed. Sufficient water must have been available, as abundant crops of corn, barley, and beans were recorded on the mission books. Because of the plentiful water and vast areas available for grazing, large herds of cattle, sheep, goats, horses, and mules were raised.

Converts were quickly attracted to the mission, and by 1776 nearly 600 neophytes were part of the community. One year later an epidemic struck, and more than half the Indians died. By 1800,

CONDÉ

Misión Nuestra Señora del Rosario de Viñadaco

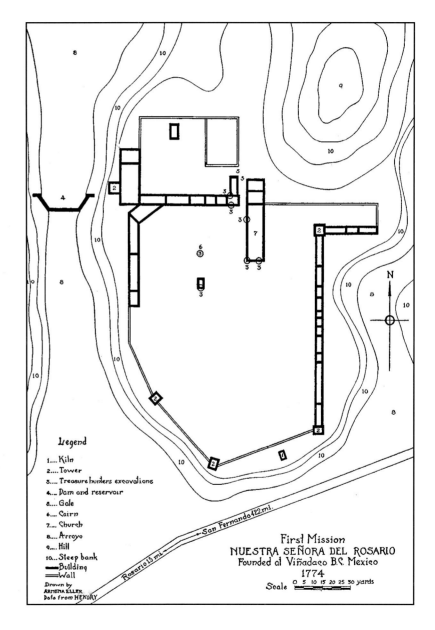

Above: *Little is left of the main east-west building, but its length of over 115 yards can easily be traced. The littered depression in the foreground falls into the gully that was spanned by the mission dam. No traces of the dam were found in 1998.*

Above left : *Many walls were still standing and the first site outline was quite apparent when this photograph was taken in 1951 by McDonald.*

Left: *The chapel is shown as it stood in 1938. This building is the extension to the right and perpendicular to the major lateral ruins.*

Right: *The plan of the first mission was taken from Meigs',* The Dominican Frontier of Lower California.

Legend

1....Kiln
2....Tower
3....Treasure hunters excavations
4....Dam and reservoir
5....Gate
6....Cairn
7....Church
8....Arroyo
9....Hill
10...Steep bank
━━Building
══Wall

Drawn by
ARMENA ELLER
Data from HENDRY

First Mission
NUESTRA SEÑORA DEL ROSARIO
Founded at Viñadaco B.C. Mexico
1774
Scale 0 5 10 15 20 25 30 yards

San Fernando 182 ml.
Rosario 15 ml.

continuing sickness and disease had reduced the Indian population to 250. Between 1800 and 1819, there were 88 baptisms and 274 burials of Indians at El Rosario. A few Indians, 18 by one count, were still living near the old mission grounds in 1860.

Even though only one-half mile from the river bottom and perennial water, the first site, as shown by the extensive development, must have proven to be ideal only as long as the spring in the side canyon flowed. In 1802, the mission was moved down the canyon 4 miles toward the sea, because water ceased to pour from the all-important spring. The site today is so arid and devoid of growth that it is hard to

Above right: *Meigs' 1926 photo at the first site shows a family enjoying their outing on the mission walls with the bells hanging on a timber frame between the children.*

Right: *In 1898, the "provisional church" was built to take the place and hold the religious objects of the fallen mission. That building, shown with a deteriorating roof in this 1951 McDonald photo, is no longer standing.*

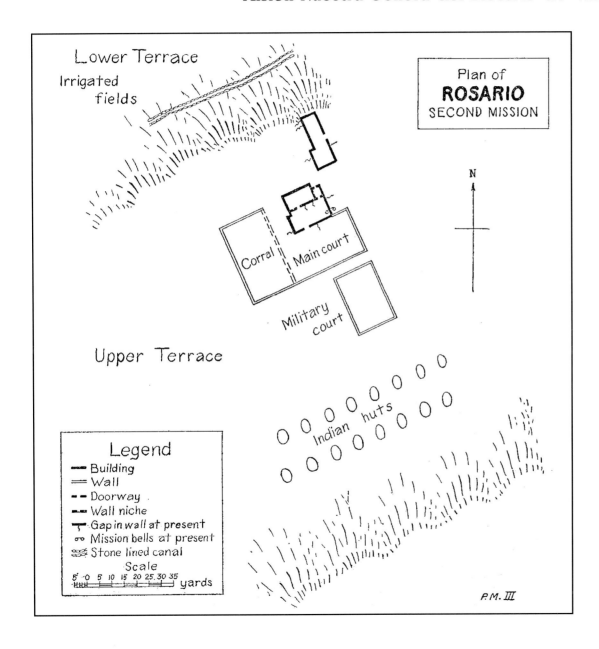

Lower Terrace

Irrigated
fields

Upper Terrace

Corral

Main court

Military
court

Indian huts

Plan of
ROSARIO
SECOND MISSION

N

Legend
━━ Building
══ Wall
-- Doorway
-•- Wall niche
⊤ Gap in wall at present
 oo Mission bells at present
≋ Stone lined canal

Scale
5′ 0 5 10 15 20 25 30 35
yards

P.M. III

imagine it as a once attractive and viable location. Some of the original adobe walls still stand, but the site has been surrounded by housing and urban clutter, including scrapped autos. Today, no one recalls the slightest water flow in the gully except during infrequent and torrential storms.

The downstream second site, sometimes called *abajo*, provided easier access to the river, more flat land for crops, and closer proximity to the sea and its bounty of clams, oysters, and fish. Also, on the Pacific coast, conveniently located Punta Baja provided shelter for the ships that carried on trade with the mission.

The new complex, which was much smaller and included far fewer structures than the first, was also built of adobe.

Meigs' map clearly shows that the second site was far smaller than the first. Even though the area was much better adapted to farming, the steady decline of the Indian population must have dictated a less ambitious building program.

In spite of the steadily declining labor force, a substantial church, storerooms, and housing for both the priests and soldiers were built. The second mission was not built as a fortification with defensive walls and guard towers, as was the first. Also, it appears that the natives were housed in nearby huts rather than in the mission enclosure.

In spite of the agreeable and productive location, *Misión Nuestra Señora del Rosario* continued to decline when ever-present European diseases decimated the native population. A resident priest may have served until 1832, at which time the mission was left to the care of the townspeople and was occasionally served by a visiting priest.

An interesting facet of El Rosario's post-mission history is that it is the location where stragglers from the private army of the American "general," William Walker, were captured and executed. In 1853, Walker had raised a force of adventurers who had tried to "conquer" Baja California by force and to establish a new nation under his questionable leadership.

CONDÉ

The mission bells, El Rosario (1800) on the left and Santa Rosa (1738) on the right, are examined by Bruce de Bourbon-Condé (center) and his party in 1938.

Misión Nuestra Señora del Rosario de Viñadaco

American photographer Charles Turrill pictured the melting second mission below the graveyard. As the "provisional church" had not yet been built, the photograph must have been taken before 1898.

The village of El Rosario grew slowly after the mission period and includes descendants of the mission soldiers and the few Indians who survived the mission era. The town is now a pleasant stop on the "Baja Highway," where wonderful lobster burritos may be obtained at Mama Espinosa's, a place made famous by the "Baja 500" road racers.

Interesting racing mementos and geological artifacts may be viewed at the restaurant. The museum near the second site of the mission displays old bells and other treasures from the long abandoned mission church.

Misión Nuestra Señora del Rosario de Viñadaco

CONDÉ

These worshipers kneel, in 1938, before the altar in the "provisional church" built in 1898. The statuary, silver cross, and other altar adornments were saved from the mission church.

1774 – 1828

Visita San José de Magdalena

FATHER JOAQUÍN VALERO, O.P.

N 27º 03.834'   W 112º 13.292'

VERNON, 1998

The lovely little stone chapel is almost intact and still survives because of its sturdy construction and isolation.

Visita San José de Magdalena

he *arroyo* San José de Magdalena, with fertile land and many Indian *rancherías,* was first considered an attractive mission site by Father Consag during the Jesuit era. Development as a Franciscan mission or farm was proposed in 1771 by Father Palóu, made urgent by a flood that nearly destroyed the mission and crops at nearby *Mulegé.* The site became a *visita* when permanent buildings and an irrigation works were started in 1774 under the Dominicans.

A stone chapel was built in the arroyo, 10 miles west of the Sea of Cortés, on a volcanic shelf at palm-top height. Sharply below, the canyon bottom is choked with palms, reeds, shrubs, and vinery lining the perennial stream.

MATHES, 1967

Little change has taken place in the 30-year span between the chapel photographs above and to the left.

A window in the chapel sidewall shows the fine masonry with chink construction that used a minimum of very valuable mortar. The log used as a lintel still survives, dried and hardened by the desert heat.

Visita San José de Magdalena

The chapel facade is made of local volcanic stone set in mortar. Note the plaster patch clinging to the wall next to the arched doorway. Some unknown preservationist has braced the doorway jambs with a palm trunk. The structure is amazingly sound and appears as if it might stand another 250 years.

The stone chapel measures 22 by 60 feet, and part of one sidewall stands to its original height of 10 feet. All four walls are of stone, some laid in mortar. Four courses of adobe bricks were laid on top of the stone to increase the height of the south sidewall. Light to the interior was provided through each sidewall by a small window. The arched main entry still stands intact, 8½ feet high by 5½ feet wide. Both the interior and exterior of the front chapel wall were plastered, as shown by the few patches of smooth mortar clinging to the stones. The chapel roof probably was of palm thatch, as no clay roofing tiles were found.

By the side of the chapel are the ruins of a 25 by 30-foot rectangular adobe building that probably was used by the visiting priest from *Mulegé* as housing. The walls are about 4 feet high and the door opening faces northeast, as does the face of the chapel.

Visita San José de Magdalena

Farther down the arroyo that flows toward the Sea of Cortés, a flattened area about 300 feet square contains the foundation ruins of several buildings. As there is no melted adobe or stone rubble in addition to the foundations, it is likely that these buildings had walls of vertical sticks, cactus, or woven palm strips. The still-standing end posts—palm tree trunks with a ridge pole leaning from the top of one to the ground—further suggest the use of palm-frond or brush thatching.

Perhaps these structures were storerooms, or more probably, housing. A nicely made stone-and-mortar *acequia* parallels Arroyo Magdalena and used to supply water to many terraced *huertas* that follow the bench between the canyon bottom and the steep dry hillside for nearly one mile. In some places, dry-laid boulder walls form three levels of terraced huertas.

Viewed from behind the back wall of the adobe structure, beside and slightly to the rear of the chapel, a beautiful cholla cactus garden is seen growing in the center of what was probably the house for the priest from Mulegé when visiting this site.

Visita San José de Magdalena

Little written information is available on this visita, but it must have contained a large Indian population because the extensive stonework—corrals, garden walls, *casas,* and acequias—indicate that many construction workers were required. The maintenance of the many gardens would also have been labor intensive.

Because of the perennial water and the obvious fertility of the area and considering the short distance to both *Mulegé* and *Guadalupe,* it would be very surprising if both the Jesuits and Franciscans did not cultivate souls and crops in this picturesque valley before the Dominicans built a stone chapel at this mission visiting station.

Whether or not farming was continued after the 1828 closing of *Misión Santa Rosalía de Mulegé* and of this visita is not known. Presently, however, the only agricultural activity is on the other side (north) of the arroyo in the area of the village of Boca de Magdalena.

Stone and mortar foundations lie in a flat adjacent to the acequia that parallels the creek bed. The chapel is farther west 100 yards on the volcanic ledge, about 50 feet above the level of this group of ruins. The area may have been for storerooms or housing for the Indian workers. Whether the buildings were built or occupied after the mission was closed is not known. The locals, however, call this area the "casas," and believe they were part of the mission-era structures. Note the vertical palm trunk "posts," which were used to support the ridge pole.

Visita San José de Magdalena

Right: *This fine grove of palms grow in the sandy creek bed and their crowns just peek over the ledge on which the chapel is built.*

Center: *Our guide Señora Marcelena Aguilar de Mesa leads the way through the palms and reeds that form a virtual wall on each river bank.*

Below: *The acequia was evidently washed away by a flood flowing down a now bone-dry side canyon.*

Visita San José de Magdalena

The author with Señor Mesa-Smith and his wife Marcelena, who spend part of the year at their home in this peaceful agricultural valley. Señor Smith was born in Comondú, and both he and his wife have numerous relatives throughout the peninsula. These kind people were of great assistance to us in finding the visita ruins.

1775 – 1839

Misión Santo Domingo de la Frontera

FOUNDED BY FATHERS MIGUEL HIDALGO, O.P. & MANUEL GARCÍA, O.P.

N 30° 46.249'   W 115° 56.204'

Misión Santo Domingo de la Frontera

Even though the mission's ruins were sadly deteriorating, the original chapel, the roofed building to the right, was still in use as a church.

Misión Santo Domingo de la Frontera

The second mission established by the Dominicans was sited 8 miles east of the Pacific and 15 miles north of the beautiful natural harbor at San Quintín. It was placed 50 miles north of *El Rosario* on the side of an *arroyo* that drains a widespread watershed of the Sierra San Pedro Mártir.

The site was chosen by Fathers Miguel Hidalgo and Manuel García because of the ample water available from the riverbed, and the many acres of land suitable for farming on the arroyo floor. This also was a place where numerous natives lived in nearby *rancherías* to supply the padres with souls to save and labor to develop the mission complex.

The first services and the mission's dedication were held August 30, 1775, in a cave under a massive red rock formation on the south side of the arroyo, 2 miles downstream from the final site. Eventually permanent structures were erected, and the site was used for nearly 20 years. Ruins of adobe were found by Meigs on the west side of the rock, and he believed these to be the remnants of the first mission buildings.

The present state of the buildings is shown viewed from the hillside. The chapel ruins to the right are partially covered by trees, and a mound tracing the outer wall can be seen at the lower left corner of this fall 2001 photo.

Misión Santo Domingo de la Frontera

Growth of the mission was quite slow as the local Indians strongly resisted missionization and frequently deserted the life of indoctrination, discipline, and hard physical labor. Father Hidalgo considered abandoning this, the most exposed, frontier mission, but held fast and asked for additional troops to supplement the 17 soldiers who were assigned to guard the frontier missions of *Velicatá, El Rosario,* and *Santo Domingo.*

Soon the force was increased to 27, and even though the soldiers were responsible for the control of the natives spread over several thousand square miles, they successfully pacified the area and the Dominicans were able to continue their push northward to establish *Misión San Vicente Ferrer* in 1780.

The move to the mission's final site took place in 1793, when a church "8 by 17 varas" (22 by 47 feet) was built. The ruins of other adobe buildings that would have included housing for the padres, soldiers' quarters, storerooms, and workshops may still be seen. All were incorporated into the walls of the mission quadrangle (175 by 190 feet).

MCDONALD, 1951

A stone veneer was added to this southwest-facing gable end wall of the chapel to prevent its collapse. It appears that there was a niche for statuary next to the partially fallen doorway in the center of the long sidewall.

Misión Santo Domingo de la Frontera

The stone reinforcing still stands beside these jagged remnants of the chapel altar wall.

A wooden lintel spans the broad opening in the long wall that must have been the front of the quadrangle that bordered a branch of El Camino Real from El Rosario.

A cemetery with both old and recent graves is within 100 yards of the mission walls, adjacent to a rock-and-earth berm that was apparently constructed to divert storm water rushing down the canyon from the mission buildings.

Farther up the side canyon was a small square enclosure made of stone. Meigs speculates that this may have been some sort of fort.

Acequias are located on both sides of Arroyo Santo Domingo, and originate near the site of a now obliterated dam about one mile upstream from the mission buildings. Rocks piled against the south canyon wall, bound with adobe and sticks, mark what was probably the attachment point of the dam. Cultivation could have taken place almost throughout the arroyo floor within range of the acequias.

A *horno*, destroyed by floods, was built against the canyon wall near the dam, and was used to fire limestone for cement to make plaster and mortar. As no mortared stone buildings of mission vintage seem to exist, the cement must have been used to make plaster to coat

Misión Santo Domingo de la Frontera

A view from the courtyard of the principal ruins that probably included a sacristy and storeroom in addition to the chapel.

An adobe wall that surrounded the ancient and modern graves that lie side by side in the camposanto is now badly deteriorated, but is still visible in the background.

the adobe mission walls and to construct and waterproof the acequias. Concrete pits in the area, said to be of mission vintage, consumed some of the cement, and were supposedly used for the tanning of hides.

To the northwest, about 20 miles, a *visita* called *San Telmo* was built as a mission ranch and to serve the Indian populace of the area. The development was so extensive that later visitors thought the compound may have been another mission. It seems however, that in spite of its size, *San Telmo* was truly

a visita of *Santo Domingo*. Only a few scattered ruins are left from this important mission ranch and farm.

As the mission records are quite incomplete, it is not possible to accurately know the population statistics for the large area served by the mission and visita. In 1782, before the establishment of the buildings at *San Telmo*, 20 families with a total of 79 souls were recorded at *Misión Santo Domingo*. That count increased to 315 by 1800. This seems like a small number, considering the large area of the mission's influence.

Misión Santa Domingo de la Frontera

The "provisional chapel" of 1890 had fallen into disrepair (although it was still occasionally used) when visited by Condé in 1936.

Many sicknesses, including a severe fever epidemic in 1802, continuously afflicted and reduced the population of the natives. Birth records from 1804 to 1821 reveal that only 98 baptisms took place. The last resident priest left *Santo Domingo* in about 1821, and the final baptism was recorded in 1839, the year *Santo Domingo* was deserted as a mission.

In spite of the rather meager population, large crops of wheat and corn were produced as well as other typical mission fruit and vegetables, including figs, pears, olives, grapes, and pomegranates. Salt was available from the briny sink holes around the bay of San Quintín, and sea otters abounded in the coastal areas. The otter pelts were a valuable item to the trading ships that stopped in the shelter of San Quintín to obtain salt and trade with the padres.

Little is written about the fate of the mission from the end of the mission era in 1839 until the end of the century. However, a soldier-based civilian populace must have taken over the mission lands, as the old mission walls were used as a "provisional" church in 1890 to serve the locals and to house religious artifacts preserved from the decaying mission. A modern church has been built on the mission grounds for use by the ranch and farm people of the surrounding area.

The area between San Quintín and *Santo Domingo* is now a rapidly growing farm area that employs thousands of field workers. It is interesting to note that even though virtually none of the mission-era native population survived, many of the laborers who have recently immigrated to the peninsula from the mainland of Mexico are of Indian or *mestizo* stock.

Recently INAH has stabilized the adobe walls, fenced the quadrangle, built an entry kiosk and a building to house religious articles that have miraculously been preserved from the mission era.

These remnants, and the rock-heaped graves in the nearby ancient cemetery, remind us of the intriguing Spanish history of Baja California.

Misión Santo Domingo de la Frontera

A spacious cave in this large rock formation at the mouth of the canyon was the site of the first religious services held by the padres at Santo Domingo. Adobe facilities were built here and used until the final facility was built 23 years later, 5 miles up the canyon near a more reliable water source.

1780 – 1833

Misión San Vicente Ferrer

FOUNDED BY FATHERS MIGUEL HIDALGO, O.P. & JOAQUÍN VALERO, O.P.

N 31° 19.375'   W 116° 15.547'

Misión San Vicente Ferrer

The recently stabilized walls of the church are painted with shadows from the clouds in the fresh clear air after a brief rainstorm.

Misión San Vicente Ferrer

Although the largest building complex of the Dominican missions was advantageously placed beside a wide flat *arroyo* with water and productive land, the neophyte population of *San Vicente* never exceeded 350 in any count by the authorities.

Fathers Hidalgo and Valero had wanted to establish *Misión San Vicente Ferrer* 50 miles north of *Santo Domingo* shortly after *El Rosario* was founded, but rebellious Indians forced a several-year delay, and the construction of the mission 12 miles from the sea could not be started until late in 1780.

San Vicente was probably more important as a fort than as a mission. As many as 30 soldiers were quartered within the compound, charged with not only defending the frontier missions from internal revolt but, more importantly, repelling and controlling the aggressive raiders who crossed the mountains from the Colorado River desert plains.

Serving as a way station, to support the northward march to help link the missions of Baja California with the new Alta California establishments from San

The 1997 archeological dig by INAH uncovered many of the footings and partial walls of the lower quadrangle that included the mission church. New adobe bricks were placed to partially restore some of the walls, and an adobe-colored plaster coating was made to preserve and waterproof all of the walls in this portion of the mission.

TURRILL, CIRCA 1880

By 1880, the mission had become a farmyard and the half-fallen church on the left had been fenced and gated, probably to hold livestock.

Misión San Vicente Ferrer

Diego to Monterey, was also an important function of this frontier bulwark.

As an agricultural center, the mission seemed to be self-sufficient. Wheat, corn, and beans were grown in ample quantities to provide for the inhabitants. At the turn of the 19th century, cattle and sheep numbered approximately 2,000, and several hundred horses, mules, and burros were part of the mission herd.

The tillable fields were limited to a few hundred acres near the river, watered by stone-lined *acequias* that led from a small dam just upstream from the mission. The potential grazing area was large, as it encompassed more than 500 square miles that were included in the mission lands.

G. W. Hendry, a University of California professor, produced this mission plan early in the 1900s. Although it does not exactly match the 1880 Turrill photograph, it does depict the site as well as possible without an intensive archeological investigation.

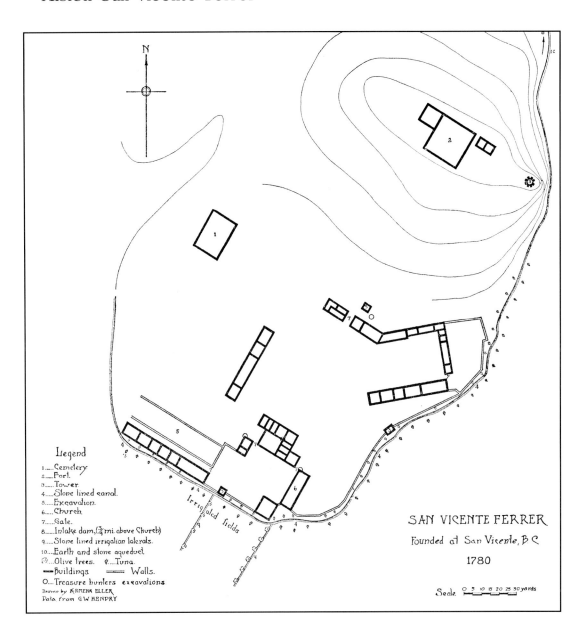

Legend

1.....Cemetery
2.....Fort.
3.....Tower.
4.....Stone lined canal.
5.....Excavation.
6.....Church.
7.....Gate.
8.....Intake dam, (¾ mi. above Church)
9.....Stone lined irrigation laterals.
10...Earth and stone aqueduct.
⊙...Olive trees.   ⸸...Tuna.
━━Buildings   ════ Walls.
O...Treasure hunters excavations
Drawn by ARMENA ELLER
Data from G W HENDRY

SAN VICENTE FERRER

Founded at San Vicente, B.C.

1780

Scale 0 5 10 15 20 25 30 yards

Misión San Vicente Ferrer

Right: *The altar end of the church, taken in 1934 from the southwest, had badly eroded when compared to the 1880 overview on page 240.*

CONDÉ

Below: *This view taken from the northeast pictures the long narrow shape of the church and sacristy outlined by adobe wall sections.*

CONDÉ

Misión San Vicente Ferrer

Left: *The church walls were braced with scaffolding during the 1997 refurbishment. They were later "stabilized" with plaster.*

Below: *Note that the broad (40-inch) stone foundations were elevated well above the external grade level to prevent groundwater from entering the raised floor of the church. This building is 66 feet long, exactly the length recorded for the church built in 1793.*

Misión San Vicente Ferrer

The foundation remnants in the foreground, uncovered by the 1997 INAH *"dig," seem to indicate the presence of a building not shown on the map on page 241 created by Hendry in the early 1900s.*

A large mission ranch was established at San Jacinto, 5 miles north of the mission. That ranch was still operating in 1934 under the care of the Aráuz family, who lived in an 1893 adobe.

The many buildings of the mission compound were of adobe with gable roofs thatched with palm fronds and brush. The lower quadrangle included the 20 by 66-foot church, a kiln, and a long barracks-like building for the single females. Across the walled courtyard were rooms for the padres, a kitchen, and other utility rooms.

Northeast of these buildings 50 yards, another quadrangle provided facilities for the military. Housing, storage and assembly rooms, an armory, a corral, and any other facilities needed by the soldiers must have been included.

On top of the hill stood a fort and watchtower overlooking the mission buildings and arroyo. An elegant modern ranch house now occupies the site.

According to Condé, who visited in 1934, the ruins of the lime kiln were near the womens' housing. The mission cemetery was located near the recently constructed gatehouse.

Meigs estimated the total aboriginal population of the San Vicente area, just prior to missionization, at 780. The diseases that decimated the other missions did not spare *San Vicente,* as almost one-third of the 120 neophytes under the mission's charge at the end of 1780 died within a year from a smallpox epidemic. The population increased during the next few years, probably by attracting "wild" Indians to the fold, with nearly 300 neophytes being counted in a census taken in 1804.

Misión San Vicente Ferrer

By 1829, about 50 years after the mission's founding, there were no Indians in the area except those few living on the immediate mission grounds, and they had declined in number to 80, including only 12 children.

Father Sales, writing of the Indians' flight from the sicknesses brought by the Europeans, said, "I can say from what I myself have experienced that many dead were to be seen in the fields. If one went to the caves he saw the dying…The heathen Indians crowded in the caves, when they noticed any infected with the disease, fled to another cave and abandoned those unfortunates, and the former, who were sometimes already infected, spread it to others…Some threw themselves into the sea, others scorched themselves with firebrands, and the poor little children, abandoned by the dead, died without help…"

The epidemics abetted by low birthrates caused by syphilis continued to decimate the natives, and by 1833 the mission was abandoned, leaving behind only a few elderly Indians to eke out a living from the old mission gardens.

The low adobe wall southwest of the mission buildings is probably what is left of the outer wall of the unmarried women's quarters. Below the wall are the remnants of the acequia used to water the fertile mission garden. Crops are still grown on this flat, well-cared-for acreage.

Today San Vicente valley is rapidly increasing in population as better water resources become available to encourage the development of modern agriculture. Many homes and small farms are scattered throughout the district.

New visitor facilities with gravel paths, a sign with the mission's history, and a few preserved walls are all that is left to commemorate the faith and determination of the padres and the labor of the Indians during the mission era.

Misión San Vicente Ferrer

The 1997 refurbishment by INAH *included making new adobe bricks from the mounds of melted adobe that remained from the original mission walls.*

1787 – 1833

Misión San Miguel Arcángel
de la Frontera

FOUNDED BY FATHER LUIS SALES, O.P.

N 32° 05.679'   W 116° 51.314'

Misión San Miguel Arcángel de la Frontera

In 1951, the ruins photographed by McDonald clearly revealed the remains of the mission founded in 1787.

Misión San Miguel Arcángel de la Frontera

An outpost north of *Misión Santo Tomás* was desired by the authorities to better link the ancient missions of Baja California with the string of new missions rapidly being completed between San Diego and the *Presidio* at Monterey.

Father Luis Sales, who was appointed to found the new mission, made two trips northward following the route pioneered by Father Crespí during his expedition to Alta California 10 years earlier. As Sales was attacked by Indians on both journeys, a strong military force was deemed necessary to protect the padre's efforts. Sales wrote that this frontier expansion was "a matter made difficult because of the harsh disposition of the Indians."

In 1787, with the aid of six soldiers from the presidio at San Diego and five from the Baja California force (probably from *San Vicente*), the mission was founded. A crude fortification and some kind of temporary chapel was built near the *estero* formed where the stream meets the sea.

The mission plan from data gathered by Professor G. W. Hendry appeared in Peveril Meigs' book, The Dominican Mission Frontier of Lower California. *Hendry's investigation took place circa 1920. The mission was moved to the second site in 1788 as recorded by Hendry.*

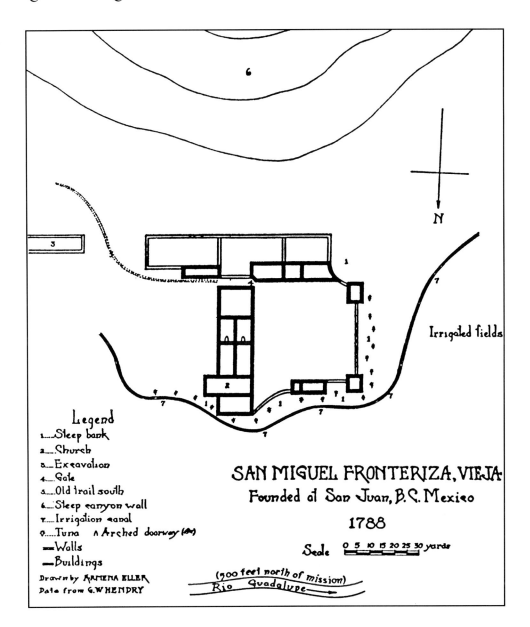

Legend
1 — Steep bank
2 — Church
3 — Excavation
4 — Gate
5 — Old trail south
6 — Steep canyon wall
7 — Irrigation canal
8 — Tuna ∧ Arched doorway (∧)
▬ Walls
▬ Buildings

Drawn by ARMENA ELLER
Data from G. W. HENDRY

SAN MIGUEL FRONTERIZA, VIEJA
Founded at San Juan, B.C. Mexico
1788

Scale 0 5 10 15 20 25 30 yards

(900 feet north of mission)
Rio Guadalupe →

Irrigated fields

Misión San Miguel Arcángel de la Frontera

One year later, the mission was moved 3 miles upstream to the south side of the *arroyo* to a site with more reliable water and ample land for crops and herds. The location was ideal as, in addition to the water and land, there were souls to save at Indian *rancherías* both upstream in the canyon and below the mission on the Pacific shore.

An adobe church, 70 feet long and roofed with red tile, was built in 1793. A *casa* for the missionaries was also built about this time. Five years later, three additional rooms and two granaries were built. West of the mission, according to Robertson, on its same small hill, stone foundation remnants indicate the possible location of a fortification and perhaps a watchtower. The last recorded construction was of new housing for the priests in 1800.

An estimate placed the aboriginal population of the area of *San Miguel* and *El Descanso* at 665 prior to missionization. The neophyte population was recorded at 117, three years after the mission's founding. The maximum number of neophytes considered part of the mission, nearly 400, was reached

Above left: *Condé's caption on the 1934 photo reads, "Ruined interior of the mission church (to right) and other room with ancient window beams still in place. From the west."*

Left: *The 1965 Mathes photo shows the additional deterioration caused by the passing years.*

Above right: *Meigs made this 1926 view from the south looking across the valley.*

Right: *A 1997 photo replicates Meig's viewpoint and also shows the protective covering INAH placed over the ruins during their refurbishment.*

Misión San Miguel Arcángel de la Frontera

in 1824. By 1829, there were 154 still surviving, and after the 1833 closure of the mission, only 25 Indians were still living in the area. As severe flooding in 1816 carried away much of the garden acreage of *San Miguel,* a new mission, *El Descanso,* was established at a nearby site with adequate arable land. It should be noted that the population figures may include the Indians of *El Descanso.* The two missions were so intertwined in function (and were less than 10 miles apart) that the poorly kept and incomplete records may combine data from both operations.

The few records available show that corn and wheat were successfully grown. Large herds of livestock were reported, with 3,900 cattle and sheep, and nearly 400 horses and mules being grazed on the combined missions' land in 1800.

The continued decline of the Indian population and the secularization edict from the Mexican government forced the abandonment of *San Miguel* as a mission in 1833. The old missions of *San Miguel, Santo Tomás,* and *Guadalupe* continued to function as churches, and by 1840 all three were served by one priest.

The site of the mission and the few standing adobe walls have been protected by INAH and are located next to a school in the attractive village of La Misión, 20 miles north of Ensenada.

Misión San Miguel Arcángel de la Frontera

Bruce Condé recorded the vandalism that exposed these human remains at San Miguel. As he states in the copy of his original caption below, the remains were then reburied.

Restos de padre o neófito desenterrados en la iglesia por vándalos en 1934. Remains of Padre or Neófito exhumed by vandals in 1934. Reburied by BC.JT

After the closing of the missions, treasure hunters vandalized graves and mission buildings in the hope of finding treasure secreted by the padres. The only "treasure" found by the padres was the faith that they had assured their converts of the kingdom of heaven.

1791 – 1849

Misión Santo Tomás de Aquino

FOUNDED BY FATHER JOSÉ LORIENTE, O.P.

*N 31° 33.513'   W 116° 24.817'

* COORDINATES OF THIRD AND FINAL SITE

Misión Santo Tomás de Aquino

VERNON, 1997

The melting ruins are the remnants of a storehouse or winery that was located in a vineyard outside the mission quadrangle.

Misión Santo Tomás de Aquino

The mission was established by Father José Loriente on April 24, 1791, in the *arroyo* of Santo Tomás, less than 5 miles from the final site at the *pueblo* of Santo Tomás.

Records indicate that 96 neophytes were quickly made part of the religious community, and that an adobe chapel of 5 by 12 *varas* (14 by 34 feet) was constructed and in use by December 1793.

Conflicting reports by competent historians make it difficult to determine which of three canyon ruins are truly the first or second mission. However, the location and history of the third and final site are quite clear.

About 5 miles from the head of the canyon, toward the sea, is a beautiful, flat grassy area of 500 by 300 yards set among large healthy oaks and sycamores. Centered in the clearing of what is now a campground and picnic area are the deteriorating remnants of an adobe building 120 feet long. As the size of the adobe's end room, 18 by 30 feet, is close to the dimensions given by Englehardt for the chapel built at the founding, it may be that this is the first site.

The adobe building at the third and final mission site has melted into the ruin shown on the facing page. It served as a winery or storage building when it was photographed in 1935. In a photo taken in 1951 by McDonald, the corrugated iron roof, obviously installed well after the mission era, was missing and the walls were badly deteriorating.

A second building joined to a wall of the first is 100 by 20 feet, divided into two sections, one 80 feet and the other 20 feet long. Perhaps these rooms were added to provide a larger chapel with sacristy or storeroom. The roofs probably were of thatch.

Even though sickness, thought to be brought on by the nearby wetlands, began to develop as indicated by a report in 1792 that stated "only 3 men and 2 women remained well," the location was not changed until mid-1794, when the mission was "removed to another site."

Misión Santo Tomás de Aquino

There, a new church and priests' dwelling of adobe were constructed. These buildings had flat roofs of poles, brush, and tules, plastered with mud.

Meigs, in 1926, carefully measured and mapped the site at the head of the canyon 3½ miles from the village of Santo Tomás. He thought this to be the first location of the mission. Fortunately he made his survey before a new road virtually obscured the ruins, located on a bench one-quarter mile from the streambed on the north side of the canyon, upstream from the junction with Arroyo Chocolate.

This seems to be the place described by Governor Castillo Negrete in 1853 when he said that the mission was founded "on the skirt of the hills on the north of the arroyo, about a league west of where it is today." It is not known if Negrete was familiar with the Sales/Ortega site one-half mile west.

In 1795, the viceroy suggested that the mission be moved to the upper plain "to avoid Mosquitos." Father Miguel López

Above right: *The photo taken by Michael Mathes in 1967 shows many of the walls standing to a height of 4 or 5 feet. This must be the spot that Sergeant Ortega, during a 1785 exploration, said was a good place for building houses, and had an abundance of willows, sycamores, and live oaks. This may be the first site of the mission.*

Right: *The further deteriorating ruins, shown in 1999, lie in front of picnic tables and public facilities at what is now a campground and picnic area. The arroyo and marsh pictured on the facing page lay next to the foot of the hills in the background.*

Misión Santo Tomás de Aquino

A small dam in an arroyo 200 yards behind and 30 feet lower than the ruins on the facing page created this lake. Upstream, the grassy marsh may have been the mosquito-breeding grounds that made moving the mission from its first site necessary.

Meigs' photograph is captioned, "The ruins of the first mission of Santo Tomás, on a small fan terrace on the northern side of the lower end of Santo Tomás valley." This caption is most puzzling as the location plotted by Meigs on his field sketch as site 1 is one-half mile southwest. Also Meigs has denoted this spot as field G on his site plan. INAH has marked this as a mission-related location.

concurred, and on July 26, 1798, wrote that because of "no progress and little pasturage," the mission should be moved. It was not until 1799, after almost five years at the second site, that the move was made up the canyon into the valley to a more healthful area with more space for animals and farming, and with several perennial springs. The adobe ruins of this third and final site now include only a few low wall sections and mounds of melted adobe.

This location, just east of Highway 1 on the north side of the village of Santo Tomás, was an extensive development. Four buildings and the foundation for a new church were built in 1799, the first year of the move. In the following years, a large church, 85 by 18 feet, a sacristy, a spinning room, and a barn were completed to form a large typical quadrangle.

Quarters for soldiers and other adobe buildings were located outside the mission walls. These and housing built for immigrants from the mainland eventually became the village of Santo Tomás.

Sadly, the few unidentifiable remains of the mission are fast melting into scattered adobe mounds. Southeast of the storehouse ruin, a beautiful olive grove borders on an extensive recreational camp, with a large swimming pool that is supplied with water from the ancient mission springs that originally served the valley as a primary irrigation source. A private dwelling by the highway abuts the old mission grounds. An original mission *acequia* borders the west edge of the mission site. McDonald reported that the mission graveyard near the storehouse was plowed up during the expanded vineyard operations early in the 1900s.

The Indian population grew to over 250 by 1800. The mission and its several ranches supported not only the native population but grazed over 1,000 head of cattle and 2,000 head of sheep on facilities as far away as the present pueblo of Maneadero. By 1849, the native population had fallen to 60. Only 16 Indians remained on the mission grounds in 1860.

Even though very prosperous from ranching, farming, and otter fur trading, this mission had a short and turbulent life due to Indian uprisings and diseases that decimated the population. Not all of the natives submitted passively to the ministrations of the padres. In 1803, first Padre Miguel López was murdered, then in the same year, Indian servants beat Father Surroca to death in his bed. In 1815, two mission Indians were attacked and killed by "free" Indians.

A priest served the mission well after the secularization edict, but the lack of neophytes made it necessary that the site be abandoned in 1849. After the departure of the mission priest, the military took over the facilities, which were then used as a fort and succeeded San Vicente as capital of Northern Baja California.

The house, photographed in 1935 by Condé, had reputedly survived from the mission era. It is possible that it is the same structure shown to the left of center in the Turrill panorama on the facing page.

Misión Santo Tomás de Aquino

TURRILL, 1886

This photograph shows the many ruins in and about the mission compound. The large building on the right is probably the winery shown earlier.

Misión Santo Tomás de Aquino

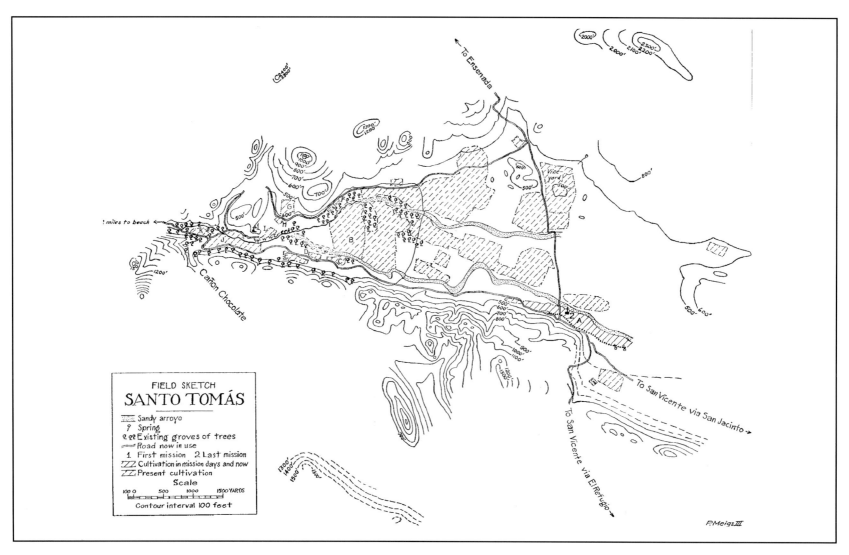

Peveril Meigs' field sketch is quite accurate when overlaid with a modern topographical 1:50,000 map. Cultivation location K is possibly the site described by Ortega in 1785 and photographed by Mathes in 1967 and perhaps the location of the mission's founding. Meigs' site 1 is 1,000 yards east of K, and field G contains survey stakes placed by INAH in 1997 to mark a mission site. G.P.S. readings confirm that Meigs' 1 is accurately placed. Meigs' site 2 is the last location, and is bordered by the present highway.

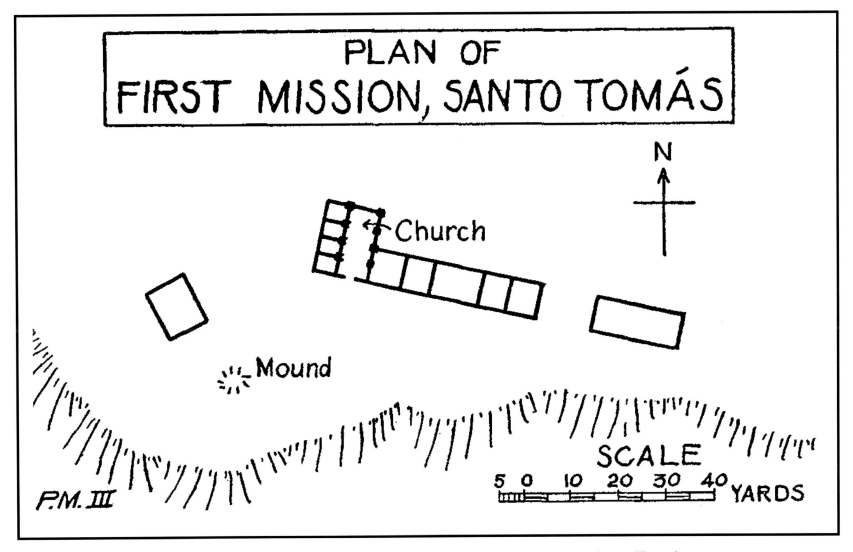

PLAN OF
FIRST MISSION, SANTO TOMÁS

N

Church

Mound

SCALE
5 0 10 20 30 40 YARDS

P.M. III

Peveril Meigs produced this mission plan and also mapped the fields at this and the last site after carefully exploring and researching the area. The coordinates N 31° 34.170', W 116° 28.304' of this site plotted on a modern topographical map agree exactly with the location recorded by Meigs on his map as site 1. They do not agree with the plotted location of field G that Meigs photographed and also called site 1.

Misión Santo Tomás de Aquino

Condé's original caption stated, "Portions of the mission barracks a short distance from the mission quadrangle. Said to have been used by the (American) filibuster Walker. From the S.   B.C. 1934."

1794 – 1824

Misión San Pedro Mártir de Verona

FOUNDED BY FATHER JOSÉ LORIENTE, O.P.[*]

N 30° 47.303'   W 115° 28.325'

[*]ACTING FOR FATHER CAIETANO PALLÁS

Misión San Pedro Mártir de Verona

C. VERNON, 1975

The meadow of La Grulla, high in the Sierra San Pedro Mártir, contains foundation elements that may be remnants of the mission's first site.

Misión San Pedro Mártir de Verona

Established on April 27, 1794, by Fray Caietano Pallás to provide a base for the evangelization of the natives who lived about the mountainous spine of Northern Baja California, *Misión San Pedro Mártir* was first sited in a meadow high in the mountains that later was given the name of the mission.

Although the exact location of the first site is not recorded, an archaeological survey conducted in 1997 found strong evidence of mission-era construction at a meadow called La Grulla, at an elevation of nearly 7,000 feet and about 8 miles northeast of the known position of the ruins of the second site.

This possible first site, called *Casilepe* by the Indians, contains "piers" one meter square made of quarried stones, and aligned in a pattern 2½ meters apart. The incomplete rectangles formed by the piers could have been the start of a room abutting an enclosure.

The Foster/Bendimez paper, "The Ruins at Casilepe," suggests that timber rather than conventional adobe construction may have been anticipated or used. It further states that additional exploration

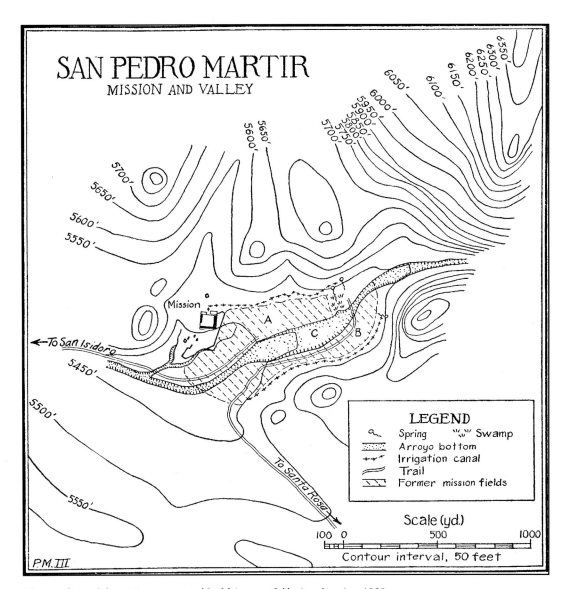

The second site of the mission was mapped by Meigs on a field trip taken circa 1930.

and study is required to determine if the meadow La Grulla was truly the first mission site.

Only a few months after the founding, the cold weather proved that the high meadows were only practical for summer pasturage. By the end of August, the mission was moved to a location with the native name of *Ajantequedo,* southwestward 8 miles down the mountain slope. Here at an elevation of 5,500 feet on an uneven, rocky brush-covered, alluvial fan above a narrow *arroyo* with a live stream, a typical mission quadrangle 65 by 90 yards was built. The mission church, a storeroom, and other buildings within the quadrangle were of adobe with red tile roofs and floors.

Acequias originating at springs on both sides of the canyon were used to supply water to the crops grown on the sides of the river bed in the bordering valley. Corn, beans, and wheat were produced on the 50 acres of this mission *huerta.* Herds of cattle, sheep, and horses were grazed on the mountain meadows above the mission in the summer and driven to the lower elevation for winter forage. The meadows are still used by local ranchers as summer pasture.

The population of the mission was surprisingly low, with 60 neophytes counted in 1794. By 1800, this number had increased

C. VERNON, 1975

Above right: *The mission's interior walls as pictured in 1975 from inside the quadrangle.*

Right: *A section of the outer wall that borders the arroyo on the south and east perimeter of the mission.*

to 94. There may have been few *rancherías* to supply potential converts in this rugged mountain terrain, or perhaps the natives of this area were independent and able to sustain themselves without the foodstuffs typically offered by the padres to encourage "reduction."

As the mission often suffered attacks by the Indians, walled cannon emplacements were used for protection. Also, accounts reveal that "runaways" created problems, as was the case in other Dominican missions.

The rate of decline of the population after 1800 is unknown, as no records regarding births and deaths are available. The date of abandonment is listed as 1806 by one knowledgeable historian, while another believes 1824 is a more reliable date. On the closing of *San Pedro*, the remaining Indians were moved to *Misión Santo Domingo*.

During the author's 1977 backpack trip to the site, only a few stone-and-earth walls, short sections of the water distribution system, and a few pieces of broken tile were found. Surely a "dig" at this mountain *arroyo* would be very productive and reveal many more clues to life at this remote mission.

According to recent reports, locating this site is quite difficult as the faint trails that led to the mission from the meadows above are overgrown, and the approach from below starting at the deserted *rancho* of San Isodoro is difficult. Finding the ruins of the interesting remnants of the Dominican's only mountain mission could best be done with the aid of a local cowboy.

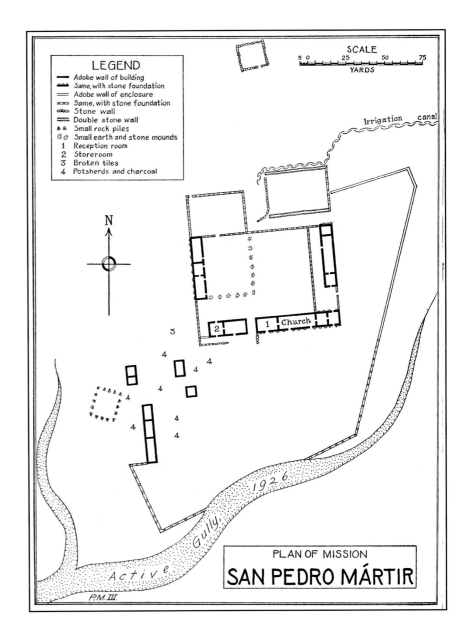

LEGEND
— Adobe wall of building
▲▲▲ Same, with stone foundation
= Adobe wall of enclosure
✕✕✕ Same, with stone foundation
◻◻◻ Stone wall
≡≡≡ Double stone wall
& & Small rock piles
✳✳ Small earth and stone mounds
1 Reception room
2 Storeroom
3 Broken tiles
4 Potsherds and charcoal

SCALE
5 0   25   50   75
YARDS

Irrigation canal

N

3

2 1 Church

4 4 4 4

Active Gully 1926.

PLAN OF MISSION
SAN PEDRO MÁRTIR

P.M.III.

Misión San Pedro Mártir de Verona

C. VERNON, 1977

Cowboys use this shack, located at the narrowing eastern end of the former mission garden marked A on Meigs' map, as shelter during the mountain grazing season. The mission springs originate from the hillside above the cabin.

1797 – 1840

Misión Santa Catalina Virgen y Mártir

FOUNDED BY FATHER JOSÉ LORIENTE, O.P.

N 31° 39.483'   W 115° 49.752'

Misión Santa Catalina Virgen y Mártir

VERNON, 2000

Looking northeastward over the footprint of the mission toward the Sierra Juárez.

Misión Santa Catalina Virgen y Mártir

Located on the path of an ancient Indian trading trail, *Misión Santa Catalina Virgen y Mártir* was founded the 12th of November, 1797, by the Dominican priest Father José Loriente. The site was chosen primarily because of its strategic location to the west of the pass of Portezuelo, through which the trail led to the desert and the Colorado River. This delta area was inhabited by *Yuman* Indians, including the *Cocopah, Kiliwa,* and *Quechan,* who were fiercely protective of their lands, and had for centuries used the trail to bring goods westward to trade with the tribes that inhabited the plains and Pacific slope of Northern Baja California.

As the Indians from the Colorado River and delta area resisted missionization and frequently raided the established Dominican coastal missions, it was necessary that *Santa Catalina* serve as a fort to control the trail and prevent the raiders from reaching the coast. It also served as a base for Spanish territorial expansion ambitions eastward to the Colorado River and, of course, as a base for Christianizing the Indians of the surrounding Alamo plain and nearby foothills of the Sierra Juárez.

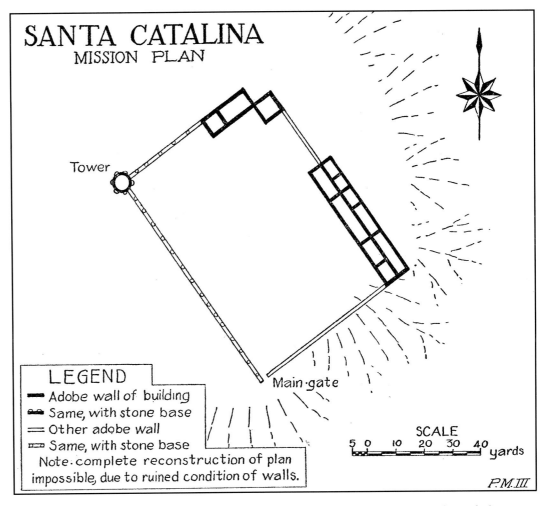

SANTA CATALINA
MISSION PLAN

Tower

Main·gate

LEGEND
- Adobe wall of building
- Same, with stone base
- Other adobe wall
- Same, with stone base

Note·complete reconstruction of plan impossible, due to ruined condition of walls.

SCALE
5 0 10 20 30 40 yards

P.M.III

Although difficult to photograph, the remains of the tower on the western corner of the plan can be discerned when standing on the site. The adobe lumps in the photograph to the left are probably the melted mounds of the rooms mapped on the north corner of the plan.

Misión Santa Catalina Virgen y Mártir

In 1794, three years before the mission was established, Sergeant José Manuel Ruiz and a military party, accompanied by Father Tomás Valdellón, visited the area and recorded it as a potential mission site. Several other expeditions, including one led by the famous José Joaquín de Arrillaga, then temporary governor of Lower California, confirmed that *Santa Catalina* was the best choice because of its water, many Indians, and its proximity to the trail to the Colorado River.

The mission locale is at an elevation of 3,500 feet on the Alamo plain and is bordered by the foothills of the Sierra Juárez. The structures were located on a knoll next to a small rocky creek that was dammed by the padres for an irrigation works. A walled rectangle, 250 by 180 feet, was constructed on stone foundations. A watchtower, 20 feet in diameter, was erected on one corner. The enclosed buildings included an adobe chapel, living quarters for the padre, storage rooms, barracks for the soldiers, and probably facilities for housing the mission Indians.

The remnants of the western and northern walls of the mission join at the round outline of the footing for the observation tower, marked by the adobe mound at the far end of the foundation trace.

Misión Santa Catalina Virgen y Mártir

By 1824, the Indian population of the mission had grown to 600 and the area of the mission's influence covered hundreds of thousands of acres that included 11 Indian *rancherías*. At this time, *Santa Catalina* was the most populous of all the Dominican missions. Cattle, sheep, horses, mules, and goats were raised, although the herds were frequently stolen by raiding Indians from the Colorado delta area.

The nearby fields were also farmed, but the undependable availability of water and the limited flat land that could be irrigated by gravity flow from the dams produced, according to mission records, only meager amounts of wheat and other crops.

The number of soldiers at the mission is not accurately known. However, as the mission plan included quarters that could have easily accommodated a dozen men, perhaps about that number was available to patrol this vast country to attempt to prevent raids by marauders.

Above right: *Rocks and stones mounded on the graves from as far back as the mission era protect the remains from desert predators. Modern concrete-covered burial places mark recently departed members of the community.*

Right: *This photo is particularly interesting as three eras of building styles are shown. The brush-and-thatch room is built of typical and traditional methods and materials. The adobe wall represents the mission-era type of construction, while the concrete block structure uses modern materials.*

Misión Santa Catalina Virgen y Mártir

In 1840, an organized raid by the *Yumans* and *Cocopás* destroyed the mission. Records indicate that 16 Indian neophytes were killed in the raid and the mission burned. After the brush-covered roofs of the adobe mission buildings had been destroyed and other buildings of wood and sticks burned, the rains quickly began to melt the adobe walls. A punitive expedition, led by Mexican soldiers accompanied by loyal Indians, was launched after the destructive attack of the rebels. The Indians who had fled to the Sierra San Pedro Mártir, many miles southeast of the mission site, were assumed to be the marauders and were killed by the pursuers.

Little physical evidence is left to aid in visualizing what must have been a busy community of clergy, soldiers, and Indians, except for the mounds outlining the foundations of the mission buildings and fortifications.

Santa Catarina, as the small *Paipai* village is now called, occupies the old mission lands, including thousands of acres to the east. Cattle and livestock are grazed, and a bit of farming is practiced to provide for local subsistence.

Margarita Castro Albáñez, a local Paipai potter, proudly displays her handmade typical "ollas." Margarita is standing on the low mound of the mission foundations.

Misión Santa Catalina Virgen y Mártir

The village of nearly a dozen homes includes a modern Catholic church, a school, and a clinic. Beautiful pottery is produced in the traditional manner by a few of the village women. The men tend the irrigation system and herd stock.

The *Paipai* is one of several tribes that makes up the small Baja California indigenous population of about 1,200. These peoples are all that remain from a total peninsular native population of nearly 50,000, including dozens of tribal groups that thrived before the coming of the Spanish in the 16th century.

Above right: *The corral, photographed from the mission site, lies on a flat that was probably cultivated in the mission era. The view looks northeastward toward the Sierra Juárez.*

Right: *Arthur North took this photograph in 1905. He titled it, "Pais Indians and typical dwelling." He further indicated that he was the first white man whom they had ever seen in their ranchería. As North spent considerable time in El Alamo, a mining camp 20 miles from Santa Catarina, the photo probably pictures the ancestors of the present Santa Catarina Paipai.*

Misión Santa Catalina Virgen y Mártir

The village of Santa Catarina is served by this small Catholic church built in the early 1980s.

1817 – 1834

Misión El Descanso

FOUNDED BY FATHER TOMÁS DE AHUMADA, O.P.

N 23° 12.281'   W 116° 54.323'

Misión El Descanso

This pretty modern church is built on the mission site, and in fact is placed directly on top of the tile floor of a now-melted mission building.

Misión El Descanso

Even though sometimes thought to be a *rancho* of *Misión San Miguel* and occasionally called *San Miguel la Nueva, El Descanso,* only 8 miles to the north, is generally considered to have been a separate mission.

Chosen in 1817 by Father Ahumada to replace the land lost by severe flooding and erosion at *San Miguel,* the site for *El Descanso* offered fine land for crops, grazing livestock, and proximity to the sea with its bounty of fresh fish, clams, and scallops. Suitable acreage was also found farther up the canyon for an orchard and vineyard.

On a hill on the south side of the *arroyo,* Meigs describes a rectangular stone foundation, 100 by 115 feet, that surrounds a smaller, barely discernible adobe ruin 36 feet square, thought to be a fort. Condé, who explored all of the Dominican missions in 1934 and

The photo at above right, taken circa 1926 by Meigs, clearly shows the shape and form of what was probably the 1830 mission church. The disintegration caused by 25 additional years of exposure to the weather is indicated by McDonald's 1951 photo to the right. Now only a mound of adobe remains on the brow of the hill.

Misión El Descanso

The shadow of the tower of the new church falls on the old mission tile floor on the north side of the building. The vertical cuts at the periphery of the tile floor, made during a 1997 exploratory dig by INAH, expose the pattern of the adobe bricks and shell-laden mortar.

Part of the area north of the church excavated by INAH reveals round river rocks set into a deep trench to form a yard-wide building foundation. The whole area is covered by a low mound of adobe formed by melted mission walls.

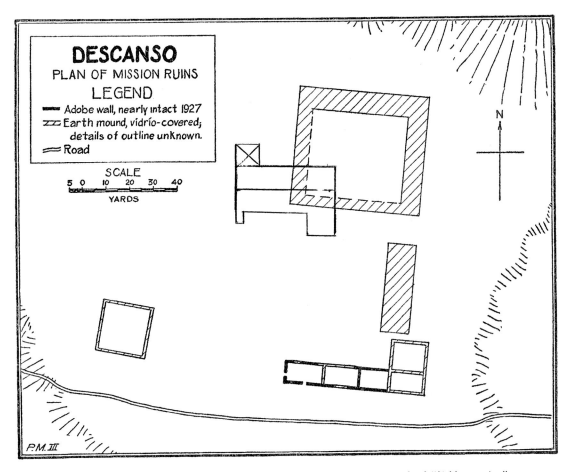

DESCANSO
PLAN OF MISSION RUINS
LEGEND
▬▬ Adobe wall, nearly intact 1927
▨▨ Earth mound, vidrío-covered;
    details of outline unknown.
═ Road

SCALE
5 0   10   20   30   40
YARDS

N

P.M.III

Meigs indicates that because of the severe degradation of the ruins, his map must be considered "highly tentative." The modern church at the site has been drawn on the quad of Meigs' map by estimating its relationship to the surrounding ruins. A commercial nursery operation with large plastic-covered greenhouses borders the new church and mission ruins on the west.

interviewed many of the locals, thought that the first site of the mission, built in 1817, was located in or near the fort. The mission records are so incomplete that it is impossible to determine if this is correct with any degree of certainty.

The buildings at the second site were placed on a low rolling hill on the north side of the arroyo. All were built of adobe and seemed to have had both tile roofs and floors. Father Félix Caballero was responsible for the 1830 construction of this complex, and managed *San Miguel* from this location.

Generous crops of wheat were obtained by dry farming methods, and large herds of cattle and sheep grazed on the hilly mission grasslands. Several miles up the arroyo, a garden, vineyard, and orchards were placed and irrigated, using a typical mission system, including a reservoir and gravity, to conduct water to the fields in open *acequias*.

El Descanso's function as a mission ceased in 1834 concurrently with *San Miguel*. By 1853, the mission was deserted and the ruins were used for storage and to pen livestock.

Misión El Descanso

It appears that the padre's dog managed to step into the wet tiles before they were fired.

1834 – 1840

Misión Nuestra Señora de Guadalupe del Norte

FOUNDED BY FATHER FÉLIX CABALLERO. O.P.

N 32° 05.445'   W 116° 34.571'

Misión Nuestra Señora de Guadalupe del Norte

VERNON, 1998

No ruins are visible on this low hill overlooking the arroyo of Río Guadalupe, although excavation would surely reveal the mission's stone foundations.

Misión Nuestra Señora de Guadalupe del Norte

The last and shortest-lived of the nine Dominican missions built in Baja California, *Guadalupe* had a turbulent and interesting life. Located 15 miles due east of *Misión San Miguel* in a beautiful valley well suited to agriculture, *Guadalupe* was established in June 1834 by Father Félix Caballero, president of the declining Baja California missions.

The buildings, probably of adobe, were placed on a low knoll 50 feet above the fertile valley floor. A stream that frequently sank below the sandy surface of the river bed provided ample water for vegetables and fruit, including olives, pears, and, of course, grapes. The valley also produced large crops of wheat in the mission days, as it did nearly a century later for the Russian immigrants.

Several mission farms and ranches were developed in the valley and the herds of cattle were the largest found anywhere in Lower California.

A village called El Povenir, adjacent to the former lands of *Misión Guadalupe*, is bordered by extensive vineyards cultivated by a corporate Mexican vintner.

McDonald's 1951 photo, taken from the same site as the more southerly pointed picture on the facing page, shows the few remnants of the mission that stood on this lovely knoll. All traces of the walls have melted away.

Misión Nuestra Señora de Guadalupe del Norte

Little information is available on the mission structures. There are no mission books describing the buildings, and only visual exploration provides what data now exists.

Meigs, in 1926, wrote of "a single angle of stone foundations, its two arms sixty and thirty yards in length respectively, close to the edge of the meseta. Within the angle are numerous pieces of red floor tiles." A few melted adobe walls appear to be shown in the 1951 photo by McDonald on page 285. No remnants of tile or adobe walls remain. Only a fence installed by INAH, and a sign describing the history of the mission, now mark the site.

Estimates indicate that about 400 Indians came under the jurisdiction of the mission. Most lived in *rancherías* along the valley floor near Río Guadalupe. The valley was called *Ojá-cuñurr* by the natives, after a large granite boulder covered with ancient hieroglyphics 1,000 yards northeast of the mission site.

Persistent rebellions by local Indians and raids by aggressive tribes from the Colorado River area plagued the mission

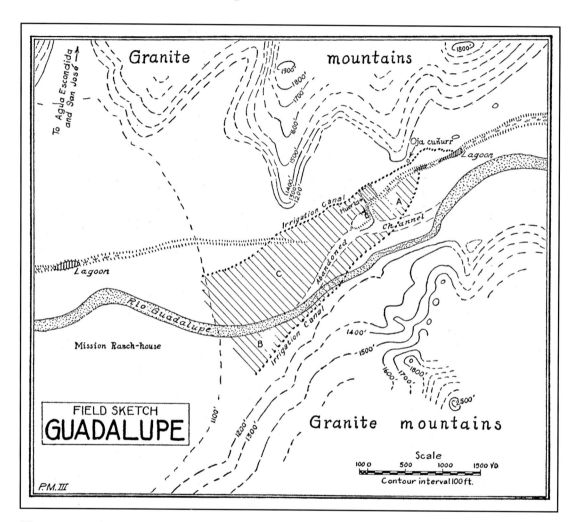

The mission site above the gardens and the location of the irrigation canals was carefully mapped by Meigs in 1926. Today, the fields farmed by the descendants of Russian immigrants extend several miles west, and are irrigated by deep well pumps rather than stone-lined canals.

Misión Nuestra Señora de Guadalupe del Norte

The concrete base in the foreground must have supported a flagpole that may have been placed to mark the location of the mission ruins. Although the stone structure in the rear was built on the mission site, it is not of mission vintage.

throughout its life. Meigs believed that the rebellions were caused by "harsh treatment at the missions."

In 1837, *Yuman* Indians from the northeast attacked and caused severe damage. The final rebellion was led by an Indian leader named Jatñil who had previously defended the missionaries. Aggravated by forced baptism and "enslavement," his armed group made an attack in 1840 and forced Father Félix Caballero to abandon the site.

Never reoccupied, the damaged buildings began to disintegrate; the abundant rainfall of this area hastened the process. Further, the damage caused by excavations of treasure hunters made the discovery of the mission's original plan virtually impossible.

Many of the local Indians continued to live in the valley after the abandonment of the mission, raising small gardens and working at the former mission cattle ranches that survived many years later. As late as 1900, there were some 400 Indians living in this manner a few miles upstream from the mission at a ranchería called *Rincón*.

After secularization, the mission lands were taken over by the Mexican government, and eventually "granted" or sold to a well-connected citizen.

Ownership of the old mission property of 13,000 acres changed hands several times until 1905, when a Russian religious sect called Molokans (milk drinkers) purchased this huge tract. Pacifists, the Molokans fled Czarist Russia to escape military service and to practice their communal, agrarian lifestyle.

Because of their industry and farming skills, the Molokans prospered and made their beautiful valley into a collection of model farms. They also migrated to Ensenada and Los Angeles, where they became integrated into their new communities. A few Molokan farms still survive on the old mission grounds, and many local families are a blend of Mexican and Molokan stock.

At the pueblo of El Povenir, the only reminder of *Misión Nuestra Señora de Guadalupe* and its Indians is a small fenced area on the knoll above the river. The fields below, however, are still used to graze livestock and raise crops.

Misión Nuestra Señora de Guadalupe del Norte

The modern headstone in the foreground replaced the more typical Russian Molokan headstone as shown to the rear. George Morzov, of San Marino, California, kneels by the grave marker of his grandfather, who emigrated to Guadalupe in 1908. This graveyard established by the Molokans is now used by the local Mexican populace.

4000 B.C.–1500 A.D.	Ancient Indian cultures left evidence of their presence by numerous cave paintings in the mountains and shell middens on the coasts of the peninsula.
1533	Cortés' ship *Concepción,* commanded by Captain Diego Bercerra, and taken by mutiny led by the pilot, Fortún Jiménez, landed near La Paz to "discover" Baja California.
1535–May 3	Cortés's expedition to gather pearls and colonize landed at Santa Cruz (La Paz). A party of 500 with soldiers, some with families, withdrew within 2 years because of lack of water and supplies.
1542	Juan Rodríguez Cabrillo sailed across the Sea of Cortés and visited Cabo San Lucas and Todos Santos Bay (Ensenada) on his voyage northward.
1565	The annual voyage of the Spanish galleon between Acapulco and Manila was initiated. San Bernabé Bay, protected by Cabo San Lucas, was later used as a rest and watering stop.
1587–Nov. 15	English pirate Thomas Cavendish captured and sacked the Spanish galleon *Santa Ana,* bound for Acapulco. The ship was burned and the crew put ashore at Cabo San Lucas.
1596–Sept. 3	Sebastían Vizcaíno attempted to colonize at La Paz near the site abandoned by Cortés.
1602–1603	Vizcaíno explored the Pacific coast as far north as Cabo Blanco (48° N).
1683–Oct. 5	Father Kino and Admiral Atondo y Antillón with an expeditionary force established a mission/fort at an *arroyo* site 2 miles from San Bruno Bay on the gulf. Abandoned in May 1685.
1687–Oct. 25	The first permanent mission was established at Loreto by Jesuit Juan María de Salvatierra. The peninsular (U.S. border southward) Indian population was estimated at 50,000 at that time.

Las Misiones Antiguas   Historic Timeline   Baja California

1709–1710 — Nearly half of the converts at the missions *Loreto, San Javier* and *Comondú* died in a smallpox epidemic.

1734–Jan. — *Misión San José del Cabo* received its first visit from the Manila galleon in search of provisions.

1734–Oct. — The *Pericú* Indians in southern Baja California revolted. The missions at *San José, Santiago, Todos Santos* and *La Paz* were sacked. Padres Carranco and Tamaral were killed.

1746–June — Father Consag explored the west coast of the Sea of Cortés northward to the Colorado River to again prove that Baja California is a peninsula, not an island.

1748 — Manuel de Ocio, who had made his fortune pearling, claimed the mining area of Santa Ana, which became the first settlement in Baja California not under missionary control.

1767–June 15 — Jesuit Expulsion Decree issued by Charles III of Spain.

1768–Feb. 3 — Jesuits expelled from Loreto, and sent under military guard to Mexico, bound for Europe, imprisonment, and exile.

1768–April 1 — Franciscans under Father Junípero Serra landed in Loreto to take charge of the 16 Baja California missions founded by the Jesuits.

1769–May 13 — Father Serra met Portolá at *Velicatá* to join the second overland journey to San Diego to establish the first Alta California mission. Serra founded *Misión San Fernando de Velicatá,* the only Baja California Franciscan mission.

1772	Father Serra's plan to transfer Baja California to the Dominicans and give the Franciscans authority over Alta California was approved by the Viceroy.
1774	The first Dominican mission was founded at El Rosario, 30 miles northwest of *Velicatá*.
1776	Loreto replaced by Monterey in Alta California as capital of the Californias.
1776–July 4	U.S. Declaration of Independence.
1800–1819	Indian burials of 3:1 over baptisms were recorded by the Dominicans.
1822–May 21	Agustín de Iturbide became Emperor of the new nation of Mexico after revolt from Spain.
1830	Capital of Baja California transferred from Loreto to La Paz.
1834–Aug. 17	Secularization of all missions in the Republic of Mexico decreed. Not enforced in Baja California until later.
1834	Last Baja California mission founded at Guadalupe, 30 miles northeast of Ensenada; abandoned in 1840.
1846–May 13	U.S. declared war on Mexico. The American military eventually landed at Veracruz on the mainland and La Paz, Mulegé, and San José on the peninsula.
1848–Feb. 2	Treaty of Guadalupe Hidalgo, U.S./Mexico; Alta California ceded by Mexico to the U.S.

1849	The Gold Rush Americanized Alta California.
1853–Nov.	William Walker, American military adventurer, invaded Baja California, captured La Paz and with a force of 45 men, and established the short-lived Republic of Lower California.
1864	Maximillian of Austria became Emperor of Mexico with armed French intervention.
1867	Emperor Maximillian executed by Juarista firing squad.
1874	Porfirio Díaz elected President of Mexico.
1878	Gold and silver mining and smelting established by the American Progreso Mining Company on old mission sites at El Triunfo. 1,000 men and 350 mules were employed extracting ore.
1883–Dec. 15	The International Company of Mexico, owned by American, British and Mexican promoters, acquired development rights to 18 million acres from Tijuana southward over 300 miles.
1885	Boleo & Cie, a Rothschild (French) company, commenced large copper mining and smelting operations and built the town of Santa Rosalía.
1885	The division of Baja California into north and south districts was made at the 28th parallel.
1889–June	British financial interests obtained colonization rights from The International Company. A pier and flour mill were built and a never-completed railroad from San Quintín to Tijuana was started.
1898	A gold rush to Santa Clara diggings near Ensenada began.

1907	Russian Molokan religious colony established at Guadalupe on old mission grounds.
1910	The Mexican revolutionary period erupted in Chihuahua with leadership under Francisco Madero.
1927	The development of the Transpeninsular highway was commenced.
1950	Baja California gained Mexican statehood.
1974	Completion of the paved Transpeninsular highway from Tijuana to Cabo San Lucas.
1974–Oct. 3	Baja California Sur became the thirtieth state in the Mexican Republic.
1975	A coastal strip on the southern peninsula at Cabo San Lucas was designated by the Mexican government for development as a tourist and hotel zone.

Glossary

Abajo	Lower or below
Acequia	Water canal or irrigation ditch
Adobe	Brick made of mud mixed with straw or other fibrous binder, then sun-dried
Alta	Upper
Arriba	Upper or above
Arroyo	Stream; may be a usually dry watercourse in Baja California
Caballero	Horseman or gentleman
Cabo	Cape, as in Cape Horn
Camino Real	Royal road; in Baja California, usually a broad foot or animal path
Camposanto	"Holy ground," graveyard
Capilla	Chapel, or small church
Cardón	Large cactus with multiple arms similar to the Saguaro of the southwest U.S.
Cirio	Slender, tall single-trunked candle-like succulent unique to Baja California
Cocina	Kitchen
Comisionados	Soldiers put in charge of missions after the departure of the Jesuits and before the Franciscans assumed control
Convento	Housing for the resident or visiting clergy within the mission compound
Cuartel	Barracks or housing for the military
Cuera	Long leather vest worn as armor by soldiers and protection by cowboys on the southwestern frontier

Don, doña	Title of respect in Spanish society
Estero	Estuary; a lagoon where a freshwater source meets the sea
GPS	Global positioning (satellite) system
Gente de razón	People of European culture, not indigenous natives
Horno	Oven; applied to a kiln for firing limestone, ore, or charcoal
Güéribo	Oak variety native to a small Baja California mountain region
Giganta	Giant, large or giantess
Huerta	Garden or orchard
Iglesia	Church
INAH	Instituto Nacional de Antropología e Historia
Jacal	Structure made of brush and sticks
Mestizo	Person of mixed Spanish and Indian blood
Muralla	Wall or barrier sometimes used for a dyke
Nave	Main body of a church
Neophyte	A mission Indian in the process of being converted to Christianity
Palapa	Shelter made of palm fronds; often round in shape
Panga	Skiff, sometimes outboard powered; the ubiquitous fisherman's work boat
Pináculos	Cone-shaped carved stone ornamentation usually placed on the cornice of a church
Pila	Water reservoir; often found at the start or end of an *acequia* or a baptismal font

Pitahaya	Cactus with multiple trunks that yields nourishing and flavorful fruit
Pueblo	Small town or village
Quadrangle	Square enclosure usually made of a church, padres' housing, a kitchen, store rooms and other mission buildings
Presa	Dam
Presidio	Fort or permanent military encampment
Ranchería	Indigenous living group, typically 30 to 80 men, women and children, usually living in a geographically defined area
Puerta	Door or pass
Rancho	Houses or group of buildings sometimes made of tree and cactus trunks and palm thatch; serves as permanent or temporary shelter for ranchers
Retablo	Altarpiece, sometimes an ornate detailed wall covering, including paintings and statuary
Reduction	The process of changing the indigenous population to mission life and Catholicism

Sacristy	Storeroom for religious articles; usually part of a church
Secularization	The legal process of converting missions to parish churches and removing their land from church control to secular ownership
Sierra	Mountains or mountain range
Vaquero	Cowboy
Visita	Visiting station, a satellite structure used as a chapel and center for Christianization subject to a mission
Viga	Beam or lintel used to support a ceiling or span a door or window opening

Spanish measurements:

Fanega	A Spanish bushel or a unit of planting area
League	2.6 miles, 4.4 kilometers
Vara	2.76 feet, 0.838 meters

Las Misiones Antiguas   Credits   Baja California

PHOTOGRAPHS

CONDÉ — Bruce de Bourbon Condé, a young Mexican army lieutenant. Photos are from the Yorba/Condé family collection and reprinted courtesy of David and Cha Cha Belardes.

CROSBY — Harry W. Crosby, resident of La Jolla, California, noted Baja California explorer, historian. Author of *Cave Paintings of Baja California* and *Antigua California.*

GULICK — Howard E. Gulick visited and mapped Baja California in the 1950s. Co-author of the *Lower California Guide Book*. Photo courtesy of the Santa Barbara Mission Archive Library.

HARLOW — Neal Harlow, former head of the University of California Press. Traveled by Model A Ford and muleback to photograph Baja California in 1950.

HENDRY — G. W. Hendry, a University of California professor. Traveled and photographed the peninsula in the early 1900s.

MEIGS — Peveril Meigs III, University of California geographer and historian. Author of *The Dominican Frontier of Lower California.*

MATHES — Dr. W. Michael Mathes, historian, professor and author of numerous books on Baja California and the Southwest.

MCDONALD — Marquis McDonald, author of *Baja: Land of Lost Missions,* who made a jeep trip in 1951 with his friend Glen Oster to visit most of the peninsular missions.

NORTH — Arthur W. North, author of *Camp and Camino,* an account of his 1905 muleback journey the length of the peninsula. Photos courtesy of his daughter Mary North Allen.

PLOCH — Thomas Ploch, Santa Barbara, California, photographer and digital image processor.

SIMONS — William H. Simons, sportsman, retired businessman, and current resident of Corona del Mar, California.

SLEVIN — Late 19th-century photographer whose pictures appeared in *Missions and Missionaries* by Father Zephyrin Englehardt.

TURRILL — Charles B. Turrill, naturalist and photographer employed by The International Co. of Mexico for their 1880s promotion of Baja California. Photographs courtesy of The Society of California Pioneers.

VERNON — Edward W. Vernon, the author.

VERNON, C. — Charles C. Vernon, retired school administrator and frequent backpacker in the Sierra San Pedro Mártir.

Las Misiones Antiguas   Credits   Baja California

VERNON, E.	Charles E. Vernon, son of the author and building contractor in Ft. Collins, Colorado.	NO CREDIT	All photographs without credit and/or date were taken by the author from 1997 to 2001.
VERNON, T.	Thomas C. Vernon, son of Charles C. Vernon, attorney and photography enthusiast.		

DRAWINGS

J. CROSBY	Joanne Haskel Crosby, artist, who reproduced and recolored the drawings of Father Ignacio Tirsch.	TIRSCH	Father Ignacio Tirsch, S.J., builder of the mission at Santiago, and artist whose paintings included Baja California missions, natives, plants, and wildlife. Drawings reproduced courtesy of the National Library, Prague, Czech Republic.
HINOJOSA	Salvador Hinojosa Oliva, La Paz B.C.S., architect and author of *La Architectura Misional de Baja California Sur.*		
HUTNICK	John Hutnick, Santa Barbara graphic designer and CAD drawing expert.	SALDANA	A 16th-century master painter. His painting of Cortés hangs in the National Museum in Madrid.
KRYGIER	Marsha Ann Krygier, daughter of the author and watercolorist living in Ft. Collins, Colorado	ZITTEL	Herman Zittel, former Forest Service employee, Southwest enthusiast, and mapmaker from Carpinteria, California.
MEIGS	See photographs. All photographs and drawings courtesy of the Meigs family.		

EXPLORERS

Many trips to Baja California were necessary to gather the information and to photograph the various missions. The author was fortunate to have wonderful friends and family as companions and interested explorers. Those people were:

Greg Cook, Joe Kulick, Tom Ploch, Bill Simons, Fos Campbell, Mike Wilken, Pancho Bareño, Joe Stewart, Jim Drain, Matt Drain, and of course the Vernon family—my son Eddie, son-in-law Jerry Krygier, my brother Clark, and his son Tommy.

MOST FREQUENTLY-USED SOURCES

Crosby, Harry, *Antigua California*. Albuquerque, New Mexico: University of New Mexico Press, 1994.
A detailed and scholarly description of the principal events and people that were part of the Jesuit era in Baja California. The most complete history of the Jesuit era in Baja California ever published. Written by a respected authority on the peninsula and its inhabitants.

Englehardt, Father Zephyrin, *The Missions and Missionaries of California* (Vol. I). Santa Barbara, California: Mission Santa Barbara, 1929.
Every peninsular mission, its successes and problems, clerics and Indians, is discussed from the viewpoint of a Catholic priest in this thorough tome.

Hinojosa, Salvador Oliva, *La Arquitectura Misional de Baja California Sur*. La Paz: Gobierno del Estado de Baja California Sur, 1984.
Architectural details including site and foundation plans of most of the Jesuit missions are well presented in this Spanish language book. The history of each mission is also briefly described in this interesting publication.

Jackson, Robert H., *The Spanish Missions of Baja California*. New York & London: Garland Publishing, Inc., 1991.
Statistical data gathered from most of the available sources is included and analyzed. The rapid native population decrease, its cause and effect, is recorded for many of the individual missions as well as the peninsula as a whole.

Mathes, W. Michael, *The Missions of Baja California*. La Paz: Gobierno de Baja California Sur/Ayuntamiento de La Paz, 1977.
A photographic "portrait" of every mission, or its remnants, supplemented by a brief narrative on the missions' history, their supervising clergy, and their Indian population. Written in English and Spanish by the knowledgeable Professor Mathes.

Meigs, Peveril III, *The Dominican Mission Frontier of Lower California*. Berkeley, California: University of California Press, 1935.
Complete and authoritative information on the Dominican missions with site maps, foundation plans, population data, and geographical data is included in this scholarly study. Also recorded is information on the Indians, their reaction to missionization, and their ultimate fate.

OTHER IMPORTANT PUBLICATIONS

Baegert, Johann Jakob, S.J., *Observations in Lower California*. Berkeley, California: University of California Press, 1979.

Bernhardson, Wayne & Scott Wayne, *Baja California*. Hawthorne, Victoria, Australia: Lonely Planet Publications, 1994.

Bolton, Herbert E., *Rim of Christendom*. New York: The Macmillan Co., 1936.

Burrus, Ernest J., *Jesuit Relations*. Los Angeles, California: Dawson's Bookshop, 1984.

Díaz, Marco, *Arquitectura en el Desierto: Misiones Jesuitas en Baja California*. Mexico: Universidad Nacional Autónoma de México, 1986.

Francez, Father James Donald, *The Lost Treasures of Baja California*. Chula Vista, California: Black Forest Press, 1996.

Gerhard, Peter & Howard E. Gulick, *Lower California Guide Book*. Glendale, California: The Arthur H. Clark Co., 1967.

Krutch, Joseph Wood, *The Forgotten Peninsula*. New York: William Sloan Assoc., 1961.

MacDonald, Marquis & Glen Oster, *Baja: The Land of the Lost Missions*. San Antonio, Texas: The Naylor Co., 1968.

Mathes, W. Michael, *Explorer of the South: Clemente Guillén Diaries, 1719–1721*. Los Angeles, California: Dawson's Book Shop, 1979.

Mathes, W. Michael, *First from the Gulf to the Pacific: The Kino-Atondo Diaries*. Los Angeles, California: Dawson's Book Shop, 1969.

Mohoff, George W., *The Molokan Colony of Guadalupe*. Montebello, California: Self-published, 1993.

Nelson, Edward W., *Lower California and Its Natural Resources –Volume XVI, First Memoir*. Washington, D.C.: Govt. Printing Office, 1921.

North, Arthur W., *The Mother of California*. San Francisco and New York: Paul Elder & Co., 1908.

North, Arthur W., *Camp and Camino in Lower California*. New York: The Baker & Taylor Co., 1910.

Nunis, Doyce B., *The Letters of Jacob Baegert, 1749–1761*. Los Angeles, California: Dawson's Book Shop, 1982.

Nunis, Doyce B., *The Drawings of Ignacio Tirsch*. Los Angeles, California: Dawson's Book Shop, 1972.

O'Neil, Ann & Don, *Loreto, Baja California*. Studio City, California: Tio Press, 2001.

Piccolo, Francisco, *Informe on the New Province of California, 1702*. Transl. by G. Hammond. Los Angeles, CA: Dawson's Book Shop, 1967.

Peralta, César Osuna, *San José del Cabo en el 250 Aniversario de su Fundación*. La Paz: Gobierno de Baja California Sur, 1980.

Robertson, Tomás, *Baja California and Its Missions*. Glendale, California: La Siesta Press, 1990.

Taraval, Sigismundo, *The Indian Uprisings in Lower California, 1734–1737*. Los Angeles, California: The Quivira Society, 1931.

Weber, Francis J., *The Missions and Missionaries of Baja California*. Los Angeles, California: Dawson's Book Shop, 1968.

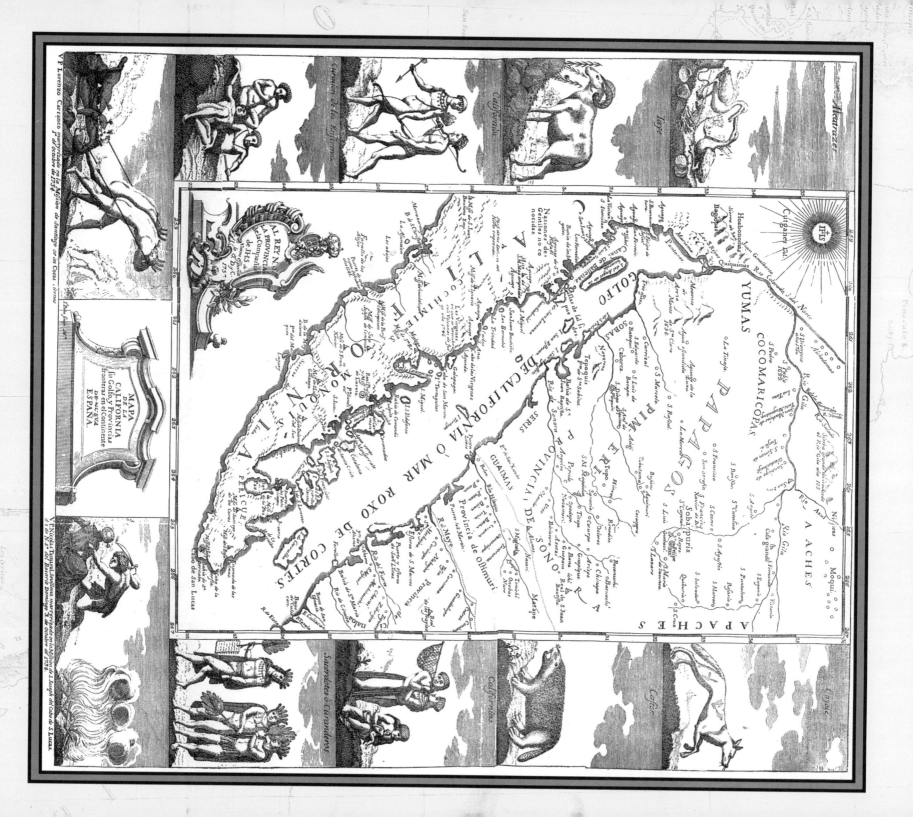

This interesting Jesuit map of 1757 shows several missions as "empezada" (started) that were never completed; several with names not formalized and at least one badly misplaced. However, the map is remarkable considering the positioning instruments of the day.